Joan Vokins, Oliver Sansom

God's Mighty Power Magnified

As manifested and revealed in his faithful handmaid Joan Vokins: also some account of her exercises, works of faith, labour of love and great travels in the work of the ministry, for the good of souls

Joan Vokins, Oliver Sansom

God's Mighty Power Magnified

As manifested and revealed in his faithful handmaid Joan Vokins: also some account of her exercises, works of faith, labour of love and great travels in the work of the ministry, for the good of souls

ISBN/EAN: 9783337212339

Printed in Europe, USA, Canada, Australia, Japan

Cover: Foto ©Thomas Meinert / pixelio.de

More available books at www.hansebooks.com

GOD'S MIGHTY POWER MAGNIFIED:

AS MANIFESTED AND REVEALED IN HIS
FAITHFUL HANDMAID,

JOAN VOKINS,

Who departed this life the 22nd of the 5th month, 1690,

Having finished her Course, and kept the Faith.

ALSO,

SOME ACCOUNT OF HER EXERCISES,
WORKS OF FAITH, LABOUR OF LOVE, & GREAT
TRAVELS IN THE WORK OF THE MINISTRY,
FOR THE GOOD OF SOULS.

NEW EDITION.

"But we have this Treasure in Earthen Vessels, that the Excellency of the Power may be of God, and not of us."—2 Cor. iv. 7.
"And he said, my Grace is sufficient for thee; for my strength is made perfect in weakness."—2 Cor. xii. 9.

COCKERMOUTH:
PRINTED BY D. FIDLER, MAIN STREET,
AND
SOLD BY H. T. WAKE, BOOKSELLER,
COCKERMOUTH.

MDCCCLXXI.

PREFACE.

"SHE BEING DEAD YET SPEAKETH,"

Is a language that seems peculiarly applicable in the revival of the writings of that devoted servant of the Lord, *Joan Vokins;* which having come to hand very unexpectedly, during a time of deep affliction from severe illness, were felt to be so comforting and strengthening in the root of divine life, that we would fain offer them afresh to the public, by re-printing and showing forth so valuable a life as was that of this dear dedicated friend; in the desire that it may lead many to consider whether they, like her, are faithfully occupying with the talent committed unto them, in humility and with godly fear; and that it may stimulate and encourage them, in this day of great declension and departure from primitive zeal and faithfulness, to uphold the standard of Truth, and Power, committed to our fathers and to us to maintain by a faithful testimony-bearing, according to the convictions of Grace imparted to all, that they may lend an ear thereunto, and be saved thereby;—all the honour and the praise belonging unto Christ who strengtheneth us.

FRITCHLEY, NEAR DERBY,
23rd of 2nd month, 1871.

TO THE READER.

Friendly Reader, the following papers and epistles here collected together, and printed for thy benefit, were not written and given forth by the will of man, or worldly wisdom, but by the will and hidden wisdom of God, which is (and ever was) a mystery to the learned scribes, and wise disputants of this world, and as foolishness to them.

Therefore, if thou wouldst come to receive the comfort, that is couched under the words and expressions, and partake of the sweetness of that life from whence they proceeded, then must thou turn in thy mind to the manifestation of the Spirit of Christ, which doth enlighten thee and all mankind, and is in great mercy freely given thee to profit withal, which gift of God is the only key that opens the mysteries of life and salvation, and reveals the things of God; which no man can know or understand, but by the inspiration of that same

Holy Spirit, which I desire thou mayst in humility wait to feel, to open and enlarge thy heart, by inspiring thee, and thereby a good understanding mayst obtain, both to discern the things belonging to thy peace, and also to savour and taste thereof, to thy comfort and satisfaction, and so to have the sense from the witness in thy own conscience, from whence the following things came.

So requesting thee to read without prejudice, in the fear of that God that searcheth thy heart, that thou mayst receive the benefit, which in true love is heartily wished thee by

Thy sincere friend,

O. SANSOM.

Note, that the following papers are not exactly placed, as to the dates, which the reader is desired to pass by.

AN ACCOUNT AND TESTIMONY CONCERNING JOAN VOKINS, FROM THE QUARTERLY MEETING FOR BERKSHIRE.

As concerning our dear friend and well-beloved sister in the Lord, *Joan Vokins*, this account and testimony lives in our hearts to give forth, that she was one whom the Lord called by his grace, and endued with power from on high, to preach the gospel of the kingdom of Heaven, and (according to her measure) her labour and exercise therein was effectual to many; and her care and diligence in her service very useful and profitable in the Churches of Christ, where she hath travelled, especially in those parts where her residence was.

She was given up to serve the Lord with her whole might, depending on the sufficiency of his Power; and did not count her life, nor any thing of this world dear unto her, for the work's sake which the Lord had called her unto; but with great courage and confidence, trusting in him (who was her sole support) she cheerfully exposed her weak body to travel, enduring great hardships both by sea and land, in the work and service of the Lord, when many perils and dangers divers ways did attend her; and though outwardly weak, she was made strong through believing in God's almighty Power. And now having fought a good fight, and finished her course here with joy, and laid down her head in peace, she is crowned with endless life and glory, to sing praises and hallelujahs to the Lord for ever and evermore. And through her faithfulness to God in her day, and valour for his Truth, and courage and constancy unto the end, she hath obtained a good report among all God's people (that knew her) in her generation. Her conversation did adorn her christian profession, and was such as did become the gospel; so that she practised what she preached, and was a lively pattern, and good example unto others in her day.

And seeing there are few that are in all things like-minded, then surely the loss of such a member in the Churches is great, and her work and service wanted and missed much among us. But seeing it is her great gain, that she is ceased from her labours, and our God's good pleasure to receive her into everlasting rest, it is our duty humbly to submit, and say: Thy will, O God, be done. And, O Lord, do thou by thy own Power raise up more such faithful labourers, and such nursing mothers in thy Israel, as this was, whom thou hast now removed.

So for the glorifying of our God, and magnifying of his Life and Power, which through Christ Jesus, was revealed and manifested in this our dear friend and sister in the Truth aforesaid, we were free to give forth this short account and testimony, with our names subscribed.

Signed at the Quarterly Meeting, at Reading, the 4th of the 3rd month, 1691.

Paul Newman.
William Austell.
John Gidden.
William Cooper.
Oliver Sansom.
William Speakman.
Adam Lawrence.
John Knowles.
John May.
William Lambole.

James Potter.
Edw. Lockey.
James Mathew.
John Fagger.
John Buy.
John Cotterell.
Abraham Bonifeild.
John Brown.
William Ballard.

The above-said testimony being read at the women's half-year's meeting for the said County, held at Reading, on the self same day above specified, and in witness of their unity with their brethren therein, and truly owning the same, did also set their hands, as followeth :

Martha Weston.
Jane Tull.
Grace Hutchings.
Mary Sandilans.
Marjery Potter.
Elizabeth Adams.

Rachel Nichols.
Mary Cooper.
Jane Ballard.
Mary Cotterell.
Marjery Bunce.
Alice Glover.

Marab Farmborrow.
Mary Baker.
Mary Buy.
Margaret Chandler.
Damaris Burgis.
Mary Austell.
Deborah Mathew.
Joan Orpwood.

Jane Sansom.
Elizabeth Wightwick.
Elizabeth Bullock.
Ann Ball.
Mary Brown.
Ann Truss.
Frances Wren.
Margaret Fulbrook.

A TESTIMONY CONCERNING JOAN VOKINS, BY THEOPHILA TOWNSEND.

I HAVE a testimony in my heart to bear for that faithful servant and handmaid of the Lord, *Joan Vokins;*—that she was a virtuous woman, truly fearing God, and one that was full of zeal and courage in her testimony for the Lord, and his blessed Truth, in her day and time, and did the work of the Lord with boldness, and holy confidence, and much cheerfulness. She stood a witness for the Truth in faithfulness, unto the end of her days, against all that did rise up in opposition, or sought to hinder the prosperity of it where she was concerned. I have known her above twenty years, and have had a correspondence with her by letters, and have been at her house, and she hath been often with me, whereby I had the knowledge of her affairs relating to the precious Truth, and of her godly care and diligence in the work of the Lord. She was of a tender spirit, ready to hold forth a hand to the weak, to help them on in the way of peace, and to watch over them for good, and encourage them in well-doing; and much delighted to see those that knew the Truth, grow up into the life and nature of it, to persevere in it in faithfulness, but much lamenting the state of the unfaithful. She had a godly care upon her for the Church of Christ in general, but especially where she had laboured, and been conversant. Her tender care was great. She was a nursing mother over the young convinced; and in her own family, great was her care and endeavours for her husband and children, that they might partake with her of the everlasting comfort, and celestial consolation that is the portion of the righteous. The Lord was very good unto her, and blessed her with a dispensation of the gospel, and gave her a word in season to speak to their several states and conditions; and the Lord blessed her endeavours, and made them effectual for their benefit, and her great comfort and satisfaction: for she was a great sufferer in the time of her first convincement among her near relations. And she was a good example among them, that by her good conversation, by the blessing of God, and assistance of his grace they were won to the Truth. Her care was great for her children, that they might come to a sense of Truth; that (she said) when she saw them cumbered, and their minds hurried with their worldly business, that she would call them together to sit down and wait upon the Lord, and sit with them, that he might compose their minds into an inward retiredness, and said, the Lord was with her in it, and often refreshed her spirit among them. And the Lord let her live to see the fruits of her labour, and the desire of her soul concerning them, and the good effect that her christian motherly care had brought forth, through the blessing of almighty God, among them: to him be the glory, for he is worthy for ever.

Her father, and husband, and children, all came to receive the Truth; and her husband is now a sufferer for Truth, under that cruel oppression of tithes, a prisoner at *Reading* gaol, with her eldest son, for the same. And when they were called to suffer, she signified to me in a letter, that it rejoiced her heart to see them willing to suffer in so good a cause. And her zeal and fervency for the holy Truth was such, that she rejoiced to see her near and dear relations suffer for it; not that she was glad because they were sufferers, but because they were faithful to the Lord, and did choose rather to suffer than deny their testimony against tithes, that antichristian yoke, which the nation groans under, the weight of which, the Lord will overturn in his own season, and ease his own heritage of that heavy burden; for he is a never-failing God to his faithful people. These things are not written only for her sake that is taken from us, but also for the sakes of them that remain in the body, that they may be like-minded with her, and be found in the same practice, watching against evil in their children and families, and encouraging them in a holy life, and judge down pride and vanity, and all superfluity, and every hurtful thing, that they may receive the same blessing, and sweet satisfaction from the Lord, as this our dear deceased friend and sister did, to the comfort of her soul, and renewing of her zeal and courage in the work and service of the Lord; who in the Power of God, went on to serve the Lord with all her might, offering up all that was near and dear unto her, not sparing her weak body, which in appearance, was fitter to keep her chamber, than travel as she did; who left husband and children, and all outward enjoyments for the Truth's sake, and went over sea to answer the Lord, and clear herself of the service he had called her unto; and he was with her, and did support and uphold her by his mighty Power, and made way for her to travel through several islands and provinces, as may be seen more at large in the following account.

She came to visit me not long before she went last up to *London*, and told me she had some papers she desired might be made public after her decease, expecting her time was not long to remain in the body, being well satisfied, that she should lay down her head in peace with God, let death come when it would. Her trials and exercises were many, but that which was her greatest grief, and heaviest burden, and most grievous to be borne, was her suffering by false brethren and apostates, who under the form and profession of Truth, did make war, and kick against the Life and Power of it; but her zeal for God, was against that libertine backsliding spirit. And the Lord bore up her head, and supported her at all times, and brought her through it all, and now hath taken her to himself out of all their reach, where *she rests from her labours, and her works do follow her.*

In her last letter, dated *London*, in the 4th month, 1690, she signified, now her service was finished, and said, I could gladly have laid down my body here among the Lord's worthies; yet seeing it is otherwise ordered, I submit to the will of my God, and do think to go homeward in a little time, or to this purpose, as if she had known her time to be near at hand; and it was very near indeed, for she did not reach home, but died at *Reading* in peace with the Lord, and in unity with all his faithful people. And blessed be the worthy Name of the Lord, she is now set free from all sorrow, pain and weakness of body, she was attended with.

And now the Lord hath taken her to her everlasting rest, out of all trials, and her peace is sure, and her rest glorious. Holy high praises to the God of all our mercies and blessings, who knows best what to do with us, and in what season to take us out of the world, and when it will be most for his glory and our good. Although we feel the want of her, and bewail our loss, yet our loss is her great gain. She was very serviceable in the country where she lived, and elsewhere; they miss her, and so do we; all that were acquainted with her, know the want of her, yet can say in submission to the will of God, *Thy will be done, O Lord.*

This is what was with me in a testimony for my dear deceased friend and sister in the Truth, *J. V.*, with whom my spirit had true unity. And though her body is removed, yet her Life is with us.

THEOPHILA TOWNSEND.

Cirencester, the 10th of the
2nd month, 1691.

MARY DREWET'S TESTIMONY CONCERNING JOAN VOKINS.

CONCERNING our dear and well-beloved friend and sister, *Joan Vokins*, who was sometimes conversant with us, and when it pleased the Lord to order her way to visit us, it was very acceptable and edifying to the sincere-hearted that loved the Truth. Her innocent life and conversation lives in our remembrance, and the sense of the loving-kindness of the Lord is worthy to be retained and kept in mind by all his people, which was largely and admirably manifested in preserving and upholding of her, through many and great exercises and trials, in her service and travels in the work of the Lord, even when great pains and weaknesses of body were upon her, which did very much attend her all along since (and sometime before) the Lord was pleased to call her forth in his service; but being borne up by his Spirit, she was given up in his will, to be at his disposal, and did not look at her own weakness, but was preserved in the true patience, having her faith standing in the blessed Power of the Lord, that failed not. Her afflictions being rightly sanctified unto her, so that she was made able, though in many pains and weaknesses of body, to undergo and perform the service the Lord called her unto with cheerfulness; and it was her joy to see friends prosper in the Truth; and although her bodily presence and speech did seem weak, yet her testimony and writing was weighty and powerful; for the Lord in the riches of his love had made her a partaker of heavenly treasure in her earthen vessel, which I have heard her often acknowledge, taking nothing to herself, but ascribing the glory and excellency of the Power, to be the free gift of God, through Jesus Christ our Lord. Her care was great concerning the young generation, exhorting them to be inwardly staid in their minds, that they might grow up in the love and life of Truth, so as to feel the work of it effected in their own hearts, that they might come up to serve the Lord, and succeed their heavenly-minded parents, who had finished their course, and were at rest in the Lord. And so now seeing it hath pleased the Lord to take unto himself this our dear friend, who hath done the work of her day in faithfulness, and is entered into everlasting rest and peace with the Lord, to sing praise and hallelujahs to his holy Name for ever, and for evermore. So desiring that we who are left a little behind, may prize our time so, as to walk in the footsteps of the faithful that are gone before, who have sought a city as faithful *Abraham* did, whose builder and maker is the Lord.

MARY DREWET.

Cirencester, the 11th of the
2nd month, 1691.

CONCERNING OUR DEAR AND TENDER MOTHER, JOAN VOKINS, WHO DEPARTED THIS LIFE THE 22ND OF THE 5TH MONTH, 1690, AT READING, IN THE COUNTY OF BERKS, AT OUR FRIEND JOHN BUY'S HOUSE.

SHE being come from *London* homewards, it pleased the Lord to put a stop to her journey, and take her to himself out of all troubles, and from her many sore pains, which her poor body was afflicted with. She was one that did truly fear the Lord, and sought the prosperity of his precious Truth above all the glory and honour of this world. Whensoever the Lord was pleased to send her forth in his service, she went without murmuring, believing the Lord would carry her through it, though weak in body; who did enable her to bear a faithful living testimony to his Name, in this her native land, and in places remote beyond the seas, as in *Barbadoes*, and in other parts of *America*, and in *Ireland*, through great exercises, in patience and cheerfulness, it being as meat and drink to her to do his will. She was one that had a great care in her family of us her children, that we might be *nurtured, and brought up in the fear of the Lord*, and have a true regard unto him, and his precious Truth, above all things in this world. This was her earnest desire and prayer to the Lord for us, that *we might be his children, that so we might truly answer the end for which we were created.*

And now, though we cannot but sorrow for the loss of so near and dear a mother as she was to us, both inwardly and outwardly, in giving us good counsel, to edification, from our childhood: but since it hath pleased the Lord to take her to himself; and considering, she hath laid down her head in the faith, and full assurance of eternal happiness, it doth out-balance all; she having *ceased from her labours, is at rest with the Lord,* who is worthy of praises and honour for evermore.

Richard Vokins, jun.   *Mary Lockey.*
Hopeful Vokins.   *Sarah Lawrence.*
Samuel Burgis.   *Hannah Burgis.*
Elizabeth Vokins.

AN ACCOUNT GIVEN BY RICHARD VOKINS, JUNIOR, OF SOME WORDS THAT HIS DEAR MOTHER SPOKE TO HIM ON HER DYING BED, VIZ.:—

Son, my weakness is great, and my pains very strong; but the Lord is large in his love to me, and good to me; he gives me patience to bear my pains, which are strong.

Ah, son! I have learned a good lesson, *Paul's lesson, in all states to be content:* and now I have nothing to do but to die. *So putting forth her hand, to take her leave of me, further said:*

Son, remember the Lord, and he will remember thee. And remember my love to thy wife, and to all my children. *And after a little stop, being weak, and her speech low, spoke these words again:* Remember the Lord, and he will remember you; and be you faithful to him, and he will bless you, and you shall be blessed.

RICHARD VOKINS.

THIS IS MY TESTIMONY CONCERNING MY DEAR SISTER, JOAN VOKINS.

She was a true and faithful labourer in the churches of God, where it was her care, that all things might be kept sweet and clean, decent and in order, as becomes the blessed Truth; she having *chosen the one thing needful, which is the better part, that shall never be taken away;* and being given up to follow the Lord faithfully in his work and service. Her prayer often in public was, that the Lord would subdue death and darkness out of our meetings and families; that we might come to witness him to be a fountain of life unto us. She was very tender-hearted, kind, and loving, willing to do good unto all, and hath left a good savour behind her; who *though dead, yet liveth.*

DANIEL BUNCE.

AN

EPISTLE TO FRIENDS.

Upon the third day of the eleventh month, 1669, as I lay very sick in my bed, I felt the everlasting blessed powerful life to arise and spring up in my heart, which gave dominion over my bodily weakness, and caused me to write these few lines unto you, that so we may consider the large love of our God, and praise his holy name together.

Dear friends, the tender bowels of God's love dearly yearns towards you all; and in his light hath he made it manifest: therefore it greatly concerns you all with the pure light to make diligent search into the very bottom of your hearts, whether or no ye be faithful to what is manifest therein: for I write unto you as unto them that know the truth, to stir you up to faithfulness therein, that the Father's drawings ye may more and more feel, and through it come to living obedience, while the

B

bowels of tender mercies are open; for if you slight his loving kindness unto you, is it not just with him to shut up his bowels of compassion? Oh how largely hath the pure God of heaven and earth manifested his loving kindness unto you! through his judgments and mercies, and through the reproofs of his instructions hath the way of life been manifested largely unto you. Therefore, dear friends, be not forgetful of his large love: Oh, let it never slip out of your remembrance; for you can never prize it to the worth of it. Therefore it concerns you all to be truly watchful the remainder of your days, that so you may see the appearances of his love, and with your whole hearts join thereunto, that no reserve may be left therein to stop the current of the pure life from flowing into your souls. And, dear hearts, it is in my heart to stir you up to feel after the pure life, if haply you may find it: whilst the fountain is open, be ye not negligent, nor unfaithful; but be faithful and obedient, that so through the faith that purifies the heart, you may draw water at the fountain of life, and feel its recourse into your souls; the virtue whereof makes the souls of the obedient fruitful and increasing in God's love, and in their unity with each other. But where the current is stopped, and the life hath not its free course, there death is over the soul, profess what they will; yea, though they may live in the very form of truth. Therefore, dear friends, in God's fear, and in the bowels of tender love to your immortal souls, I do exhort you all to be diligent, to keep your meetings, and assemble yourselves often together; let not the gain of the perishing things hinder you of the gain of that which will never perish; for verily there is none can witness a free recourse unto the fountain of life, but those whose hearts are gathered out of the perishing things; and such do partake of the living springs, which do greatly refresh their immortal souls; and it is more to me than I can express. Therefore, dear hearts, think not your time long, neither let the world hinder, but keep your meetings frequently, there to wait with sincere hearts; for those that so wait, never lose their reward; therefore be ye encouraged to wait upon the Lord, that in the pure refreshing life your souls may come to have an habitation, the which to know a dwelling and abiding in, is more precious than words can demonstrate: and let patience have its perfect work in your hearts, that all prejudice may be kept out; for where envy and strife is, there is confusion. Therefore, dear friends, it concerns you all to dwell in the patience, and in the wisdom that comes from above, which is first *pure, then peaceable, gentle, easy to be entreated, full of mercy and good fruits, without partiality, and without hypo-*

crisy. And so the God of peace establish your hearts in his everlasting truth and righteousness for ever. Amen.

I am, your unfeigned friend,

J. V.

The 3rd of the
11th month, 1669.

This to be read amongst Friends.

A LOVING ADVERTISEMENT UNTO ALL THOSE WHO JOIN TOGETHER TO PERSECUTE THE INNOCENT.

Pilate and Herod consulted together in this abominable work, and were made friends; although before they were at enmity, as you may see in Luke xxiii. And in the same chapter you may read how *Pilate* called together the high priests, the rulers, and the people, who had joined together, and falsely and vehemently accused the innocent; and when those persecutors were come (mark how *Pilate's* words run);—" *Ye have brought this man unto me, as one that perverteth the people: Behold,*" (saith he) "*I have examined him before you, and I find no fault in him;*" notwithstanding their many accusations, as you may read of in that chapter; no, nor yet *Herod* neither; for *Pilate* sent him to *Herod* to be examined, and they found no cause for what they did, as *Pilate* himself confesseth no less than three times before them all, as you may see in verse 22; and yet for all this, those wicked persecutors' enmity was so great against the truth, and their love to Christ Jesus so small, that they joined together with *Judas* their informer, and crucified the Holy One. Oh consider this, you wicked persecutors, who have set your hands to the devil's work! Did he not enter into *Judas* before he informed against Christ? O consider whose work you are a doing! and see whether the scriptures do not testify against the same ever since *Cain* and *Abel?* Oh be advised, and do not slay God's witness in your hearts, as *Pilate* and *Herod*, and the rest of that wicked crew did! for you may see there was something in *Pilate* and *Herod* which let them see there was no fault in Jesus; they had a witness for him in their hearts, which if they had loved and obeyed, they would not have slain the Lord of Life: but they did then, as you do now, rebelled against it, and counted it of no value, and chose rather to please wicked men, who did then, as you are now doing; they brought their Law to cover their wickedness; and said, "*By their Law he ought to die;*" and so they violated the righteous **Law** of God, which is light, which manifested in their hearts there was no fault in him. Oh! consider this, you envious persecutors, and turn to the light of Christ Jesus, which shineth in your dark hearts; and read your states there; and cease your evil doing before it be too late, lest the god of this world blind your eyes, and harden your hearts, and bring you to destruction, as he did *Judas*, who was a resister of the light. I shall appeal to the witness for God in your hearts, and come let us be tried by it. Have you not done as bad as those before-mentioned, yea rather worse? for you have reproachfully slandered, and falsely accused us behind our back, and caused many of us to suffer the loss of our goods, without examination or accusation to our faces; in this you outstript the cruelty of those before-named, and the heathen also; for they permitted *Paul* to be examined, and also to speak for himself, as you may see in the scripture, which you call your rule, and yet do err, not knowing the scriptures, nor the power of God; for if you did, you would not wrong and persecute your innocent neighbours, who do you no harm, but desire the everlasting good of all, even of our greatest enemies. Oh, do you do by us as you would have us do by you! Would you have us persecute and tear away your goods, because you go to your worship? or because you will not come to ours? or would you not think it very hard to be so dealt by? Oh, come and be tried by your own rule! and read from the beginning to the end, and see whether the persecutors were not the false worshipers in all generations, and the true ones the sufferers; and were not they as high in their wisdom and learning as you are, who crucified Christ, and set your original over his head, of *Greek, Hebrew, and Latin?* and they counted him of too low a degree for them to receive, and they mocked, and scoffed, and derided him, and thereby manifested their enmity against him and his followers then, as you do yours now against us.

Come down, you high-minded persecutors, and bow before the Lord, and turn to his witness in your hearts which reproves you in secret, and testifies for us; and it hath made many of you to confess to our innocency and harmlessness, notwithstanding the many false aspersions that the wicked have cast upon us; and although we have a witness in your hearts for us, yet your mercies are still cruelties towards us. Oh, do not think to hide yourselves from the all-seeing eye of the Lord! for assuredly his righteous judgments will find you out, and then all false coverings will be too narrow: Do you think your law will plead for you then, or those who set it forth excuse you? Oh no! the righteous Law of God, which you have violated and broken, and disobeyed now, will then rise up in judgment, and bear witness against you; therefore leave off all your false coverings for your persecution; for they are but deceit, and will deceive you, and stand you in no stead when you come to account for your deeds done in the body.

And now you of my neighbours and country, who resist the spirit of the Lord, and follow the imaginations of your own dark hearts, and boast yourselves in wickedness: As your forefathers did, so do you; they boasted and said, " *They had the law and the prophets, and were* Abraham's *seed, and had one father, even God;*" and yet Christ told them plainly, " *They were of their father the Devil, and his works were they doing:*" and so are you now, who are striving against those who worship in the spirit and in the truth.

Oh do not strive to limit the Holy Spirit of the Lord, which is but one in the male and in the female! Were not the scripture's testimonies to be fulfilled? Oh! when will you witness that saying fulfilled, which saith on this wise, "*I will pour forth of my spirit upon all flesh, and my sons and my daughters shall prophecy?*" [Mark]. It is the sons and daughters of the Lord that are led by his Spirit, and not the persecutors. Whilst I walked with you in the broad way, which leadeth to destruction, you did not persecute me; but when it pleased the Lord to turn me from darkness unto light, and from Satan's power unto his own, then your enmity began: but when I went along with you to your worship, I had what this world could afford of the fatness and fulness thereof; but I must needs tell you, I had leanness in my soul. Oh search and try whether it be not so with you, who have gone these many years! for I went with as much zeal as any of you; therefore let not your blind zeal deceive you: I turned not from you through enmity against you, but because that dead worship deceived my soul; for when Christ Jesus, through his love unto my soul, did make known his light in my heart, which shewed me the narrow way, which leadeth unto life, then I chose rather to suffer with the people of God, than to enjoy your favour, or all the pleasures, or profits, or honour this world can afford.

And all you that think ye are doing, as you should do, turn unto the Light, that ye may see what you are doing; and may become from persecutors to be sufferers, even as *Paul* was, through his obedience unto the Light; and he thought when he was in darkness and blind zeal, that he did as he should do: Oh! therefore take you heed, and be no longer deceived, but turn unto the Light, before it be too late; for the time hasteneth and passeth away, and there is nothing else that will stand you in stead when time shall be no more: O therefore be awakened and arise from the dead, that Christ Jesus may be your Light and your leader, as he was *David's*: for what doth it profit you to read the scriptures, or to hear of the promises or mercies of the Lord unto the children of light? This will stand you in no stead, whilst you yourselves are in darkness, and under the shadow of death. Oh do not heap up that unto yourselves, which you have no right unto! for you are in the darkness, in the persecuting state, which was, and is always blind: and how dare you in such a state to appear before the Lord? Do you think his all-seeing eye doth not behold your doings? Yes verily; and his righteous judgments assuredly will find you out; and then all your talking of that you live not in, will do you no good.

How often have you and your teachers been reading and talking of loving enemies, and of walking in the light, as Christ is in the light, and many such like things? and yet are found hating your soul's friends, who are telling you the truth, and reproving you for evil; and you are so far from walking in the light, that you remain in your sins, and plead for so doing until the last: do you think that the Lord will be limited by you until the last hour?

Oh turn to the reproofs of his light in your hearts, which maketh manifest the evil of your ways, whilst the day of God's love lasteth unto you! that through his precious judgments your souls may come to be redeemed; for it is through judgment that *Sion* witnesseth redemption, and the honest heart loveth judgment; and if you will obey the light, it will lead you into judgment; and when you come to witness, your souls redeemed thereby, then you will witness *David's* state, who said " O Lord, how I love thy judgments!" and he desired the Lord "*to send forth his truth and his light, to lead him;*" and it was his law, and he walked in it: and if you would do so, you would have the royal law of love in your hearts; and then you would have fellowship with Jesus, and feel the effects of his blood to cleanse you from all sin on this side the grave, and then you will plead no longer to strengthen the devil's kingdom; for, if you die in your sins, you will add greatly to his kingdom; for those who live and die in their sins do never inherit the kingdom of Heaven; for no unclean thing can come there, but they are for the lake that burneth for ever.

By one that wishes well to all souls,

JOAN VOKINS.

Written the 9th day of the
11th month, 1670.

TO FRIENDS AT AND NIGH *COLEBROOK* AND *LONGFORD* MEETING, AND THEREAWAY.

DEAR FRIENDS, I having you often in mind, thought it long before I could send a few lines, having kept my bed this three months or more, and have not been able to write; and I am very weak still, I could not go from my bed: but hearing of an opportunity, have in much weakness written that which lay most upon my mind, which is for the building of you up in the most Holy faith, and encouraging of you in well-doing.

Oh my dear and tender friends, feel the tender love of the God of love, that we may magnify his name together, though at a distance in person: O the unutterable loving-kindness of our God, what tongue can declare it? How hath he preserved us, and provided for us hitherto, beyond what our hearts could desire! Hath he not done that for us which none other could do? Hath he not delivered out of dangers deep, and difficulties many? Or hath he been ever wanting to us in doing us good? Oh, surely no! but he hath multiplied his mercies, and increased blessings frequently, and freely, as he in his wisdom sees what is most convenient for us: and if he please to feed us with the bread of affliction, and the water of adversity; yet let us to his teachings keep, that we may learn to profit thereby. Have not the trials and exercises of our faith and patience, brought us to a good experience of the love of our God? O let us keep a narrow watch over our hearts, that the enemy may not subtly creep in under any pretence; for if he be hearkened to, he will weaken the faith, and unbelief will enter, and then the murmuring spirit will be ready to charge the Lord foolishly. Oh, dear hearts! our tender Father is not wanting, but is a present help in all our needs: therefore let it be the whole and sole bent of our minds to perform our duties unto him.

Oh, up and be doing, for the time is come that none must be idle; but all that would have the wages of well-doing, must be faithful every one in his place, and none to make excuses; for Christ our Head is full of virtue, and strength, and might, and ready to communicate to all his members a suitable and seasonable supply at all times, and if we (as diligent servants) wait on him, our tender Master, he will discover our particular duties, and show us what is required of us. Oh let us go on with courage unanimously, that we may be helpful one unto another, and so bring honour to our Head, that we may feel his power supporting us upon all occasions, that we may not doubt nor faint in our minds by reason of the buffettings of the power of darkness; but through the faith in Christ Jesus we may obtain victory over all that would hinder the prosperity of Truth, and keep it under: for Truth must reign, and the Lord will be honoured in the dominion thereof. And he will sweep the nation with the besom of his wrath; and the hypocrites shall be tried, and fear shall surprise them, and woe will be to them that are at ease in *Sion*. But well will it be with them who think nothing too dear to part with for the Truth's sake, whose hearts are singly resigned to serve the Lord with all that he hath given them, which is no more than our reasonable duty, which we have good cause diligently to perform, so that we may daily feel the virtue of life continued and renewed to us unto the end; and in the end a double reward, which our God hath prepared for all that hold out and endure thereunto. Blessed be his holy Name for ever, and evermore.

Dear friends, feel me in that which thinks no evil, and in it receive my salutation, that it may reach unto the same in you: that we may breathe one for another, and be refreshed as members of one body. We cannot say one unto another, I have no need of thee; for there is work for us all in the vineyard. Oh let us be diligent while we have time, that we may receive our penny of life to the comforting of our souls every day; for we do not serve a hard Master.

So in that which engages to his service do I bid you farewell.

> Your friend in that which engages our hearts to serve our God faithfully without any reserve,
>
> J. V.

The 1st of the
6th month, 1678.

SOME ACCOUNT GIVEN FORTH BY **JOAN VOKINS** OF THE GREAT GOODNESS AND MERCY OF THE LORD TOWARDS HER, AND OF THE WONDERFUL WORKS THAT HE HATH DONE FOR HER; CONDUCING TO HIS GLORY AND HER GREAT JOY AND COMFORT. WRITTTEN WITH HER OWN HAND (A FEW MONTHS BEFORE HER DECEASE) AS FOLLOWETH:—

SOMETHING of the tender dealing of the Lord with me ever since my childhood, for (blessed be his Name) he preserved me from many evils that youth is often ensnared with; and by his Light (that I then had no acquaintance with) shewed me the vanity and vain customs of the world when I was very young, and all along my youth his good Spirit did still strive with me to preserve me from sin and evil. And if I had at any time, through persuasion of others, gone to that they called recreation, I should be so condemned for passing away my precious time, that I could have no peace, so that I could take no delight in their pastime, but was still condemned. And many times I cried to the righteous God to reveal his way unto me; and I promised to walk therein whatever I endured. For the snares of the world, the Lord was pleased to discover, and in some measure to make known the Cross of Jesus that crucifies unto the world; and as I inclined to take it up and follow Jesus through the many tribulations, he endowed me with his Almighty Power, wherein hath been my help, blessed be his worthy Name for ever. For his loving-kindness never fails, but his mercies endure for ever, and his great compassion and tender dealing towards my soul, when in darkness and under the region of the shadow of death, is never to be forgotten; for it hath been largely extended unto me, when in deep distress, when my cry was often, Lord reveal thy way unto me, that I may walk therein, whatever I undergo.

But when I found the way so strait and narrow, I could very willingly have turned aside for ease; for flesh and blood could not bear that which I had then to undergo; but blessed and renowned be the Spirit of Truth, my comforter, which leads unto all Truth; for when I was in a dejected condition about *Reprobation* and *Election*, neither *priest* nor *professor* could open the mystery of *Election* and *Reprobation;* but the Spirit of Light and Life (which is the Spirit of Jesus) opened my understanding, and revealed the mystery of the two seeds, how that the one is for ever blessed, and the other cursed. And also what happiness might be received by taking heed to the light that shined in my heart, which makes manifest, that the way to the crown of glory is through the daily cross to my own will, and to take Christ's yoke upon that nature that would not be subject. Oh how precious is the counsel of him who said, " *Take my yoke upon you, and learn of me; for my yoke is easy, and my burden is light, and ye shall find rest for your souls:*" and that rest I sorely wanted, until I learned of Jesus to be meek and lowly in heart, and to suffer for well-doing; and then (glory unto his Holy Name for ever) his blessed reward my soul was daily made a partaker of. Though hated by evil doers, yet loved by the Lord, and that engaged me to give up to his disposal, and to answer his requirings, not accounting myself, nor any thing he had given me, too much to part with, that the Truth may be propagated, and my tender God honoured. For (blessed be his worthy Name) he hath filled my cup with the sweet salvation of his Son Christ Jesus, the light and Saviour of his poor helpless ones, who have no other to depend upon for help at all times, but wait daily to be furnished upon every occasion to serve him in all faithfulness; for he is worthy my soul can truly say, for he gave me of his good spirit, and it was with me (yet unknown) when I rebelled against it, and was not willing to be subject to its leadings, nor observing of its dictates as I ought to have been. Oh, then did I want power (as many do now) not knowing the sufficiency of the engrafted word of God's grace that is able to save; but when I followed its counsel, I found it sufficient to bring good to me, out of great afflictions, beyond my expectation; and then I could plead no excuse, knowing that unto the Lord Jesus (who had brought great things to pass) I must give my account. For he hath manifested his power, and I have cause to believe it will never fail towards his people, if we fail not to obey the manifestation of it; but faithfulness is required to the talent received, for which we must give an account; and then what can stand us in stead, if we have not an increase? This was my concern for many years, and I could not take comfort in husband or children, house, or land, or any visibles, for want of the marriage union with the Lamb of God, that takes away the sins of the souls of those that cannot be satisfied in them; but are weary of the burden of them, as I was. And God by his Spirit shewed me, he abhorred my self-righteousness, and let me see that in him was righteousness, life and power; and then I was sensible that he is the light of the world, that enlightens every one that comes into the world; and that he was striving with me from my youth, which was before ever I heard the name *Quaker;* and then I did believe that there was a people or church over whom Christ Jesus was Head, though I could yet not find them, nor be a member of them; yet long sought after it sorrowfully, with many strong and fervent cries and desires. But the Lord in his own due time answered my weary soul, and made known more and more of the way of his Truth and people, and at length sent some of his messengers, as instruments in his hand, for my encouragement and confirmation. Then was I, and many desolate ones, right glad (whose souls had long languished) for the glad tidings that they brought with them, how that we might inherit substance which we had long sought and been searching for, both in the scriptures, and amongst professors of many sorts of professions; for we would fain have filled our souls with the husks, but that could not satisfy; we knew not the saving health of him who said, "*I wisdom lead in the midst of the paths of judgment, to teach them that love and follow me to inherit substance.*" Oh, this is that which did at first convince us, and tendered our hearts in the beginning. Then what was too near or dear for us to part with in the day of our deep distress, when none could cure our wounded souls? Oh how precious was the heart-searching light when we first knew it to shine upon our tabernacles, to guide us in the narrow way wherein is life, and perfect peace for those whose minds are stayed on the Lord! And when I have read, that he would keep them in perfect peace whose minds are stayed on him, what would not I have done, that it might have been my condition? But then I could not watch nor wait, but was as a ship without an anchor among the merciless waves; but praises unto the Lord for ever, he caused the living hope to spring that anchored in trying times. And I was, even as *Israel* at the *Red sea*, compassed all round on every hand; great was the strait that I was then in, much hardship; the sea before, and the enemy presenting so much impossibility, that his proud waves of temptations, buffettings, and false accusations had almost sunk me under. Oh then did I cry unto the God of mercy and tender compassion, that I might but stand still and behold his salvation; and he did arise and rebuke the enemy, and made way for me to travel on in my heavenly progress, and overturned the mountains that were on each hand, and dismayed *Pharaoh* and his host, (which I may compare my relations and the professors unto) for they pursued me and made my sufferings great, till they had wearied themselves. Their oppression was so sore, that I sometimes was ready to faint, and even to say, surely, I shall one day fall; but living praises unto the Almighty, he hath made me a partaker of the sure mercies of *David*, and hath subdued Truth's enemies before him, and kept and preserved me faithful, till several of my relations were convinced, that God's power was with me; and now when my husband, and children, and relations are with me in a good meeting, and the powerful presence of the Lord is amongst us, it is a blessed reward for all, for one soul is more worth than all the world, as saith the scripture. Therefore faithfulness is very needful, for it doth produce a good effect, whatever we may endure; for the momentary affliction that we meet with here, doth produce a further weight of glory hereafter, and in the sense of the same my head was borne up to endure hardships, when I could willingly have hidden or got ease; but I considered that I could not hide from the Lord, who brought to my remembrance my promise that I made before his way was revealed to me; and if I broke covenant with the Lord, I should never enter into his rest. Oh then a suffering in the flesh, and a ceasing from sin, was the delight of my soul; although the enemy ceased not, but night and day, as a roaring lion, and a cunning hunter, seeking for the precious life, chased my poor soul as a partridge on the mountains. But my God had shewed me that the way to rest was through many troubles, and that he would be at hand to deliver out of them all by his Almighty power; (but I could hardly trust it then;) but yet, turning to it, I found preservation by it, when the backsliding of some had like to have caused me to stumble. The unerring Spirit of Jesus shewed me that if thousands fall on the one hand, and tens of thousands on the other, that should not defile me; and if all the rest were righteous, that should not justify me, if I did not obey the Truth, now he had made known his covenant of life, which I so deeply engaged to be faithful unto. And then I turned my back on the world, and all the friendship and glory of it, that I might obtain the favour of Jesus, who condemned me for my self-righteousness, as for my known sins, for I was cautious of sinning against the Lord ever since my youth, and desired after the best religion and company; and when I was very young in years, I greatly delighted to go to professors' meetings, and could bring home the text, and repeat much of their sermons, but yet that brought no benefit to my poor hungry soul. And when I was in secret, before the all-seeing eye of the Lord, he administered condemnation upon it all, and I had no peace inwardly; although none could condemn me for any misdemeanor, as outwardly; but when my own righteousness became loathsome to me, then was I made willing to part with all that had been near and dear unto me, that I might feel and witness the robe of Christ's righteousness revealed, and be clothed therewith. And as for my husband and children, my true and tender love was so great, that I could have done or suffered much for them ; but if I had disobeyed the Lord, to please them, I might have provoked him to have withholden his mercies from us all, and to bring his judgments upon us ; and then who shall excuse in the day of account? Then if a man (as the scripture says) should give the fruit of his body for the sin of his soul, it will not be accepted. Then husbands, and wives, and parents, and children, and servants, shall all receive according to their doings; and none that disobey the Lord can be excused, no more than *Adam* was, when he said, That the woman gave him the forbidden fruit, and he did eat, and so provoked the Lord, that the curse came upon himself, and could not be excused. And although man and wife should be helpful one to another in righteousness, yet too many there are, since the fall, that hinder and hurt each other, for which an account must be given unavoidably. And this did I consider many times, and earnestly endeavour to avoid; notwithstanding the false aspersions that might arise, yet I still endeavoured to keep my conscience clear in the sight of my tender God ; and none can lay any thing to my charge, except it be for serving the living and true God, though in that way that many may call *heresy*, yet I do worship him in spirit and in truth. For as Christ Jesus hath said, it is come to pass, that our heavenly Father seeketh such, and always sought such to worship him, in his own spiritual way of worship; which shall stand, when all idolatry and invented worships shall fall.

The 1st month, 1680. Written on board the first ship as I went to *New England*, when none that saw me, expected my life; but the Lord was with me, and relieved me, and his blessed power raised me, as at many other times.

And I arrived at *New York*, the 4th day of the 3rd month, 1680, and a maiden friend, whose name was *Sarah Yoklet*, went with me from *England*, and travelled with me until I came to *Oyster Bay*, in *Long Island*; and the Lord so ordered it, that when she left me, another woman-friend, that had a testimony, was my companion several months, whose name was *Lydia Wright*.

Oh matchless mercies of the Lord, who can rightly consider them as they have been manifested, and not be tendered, as I am! Oh how long did his tender Spirit strive with me before I gave up to go to sea! How did his long patience wait and suffer! Surely it is worthy to be remembered; for he might have cut me off in a disobedient condition: but blessed and magnified be his heart-tendering power; it bowed me from year to year, and brought me into subjection, when in a low condition I could not help myself, and had no other to help me. Oh then did it support me in exercises, sore both in body and spirit; when my mind hath been so dejected, that my faith almost failed, then did my tender Father, through the Son of his love, Christ Jesus, yield me sweet relief, though in a weary land, and sweetly encouraged me to travel on. And many sweet promises, which before he gave me, as I stood singly resigned to obey his commands, and be at his disposal, he was never wanting to fulfil; but by sea and land hath multiplied his mercies, *and renewed a right spirit in me,* to the resolving of doubts, and casting out of false fears (everlasting praises to his most holy Name); for often did that cause torment, when the dark reasoner was very busy. Then did I cry unto the Lord, and say, Surely thou knowest all, and I have none but thee to help, many eyes are over me, great difficulties surround me on every hand, and I am the poorest and weakest that I do know; and if I should fail by the way, how would the enemy rejoice, and the truth be reproached? And much buffetting did I undergo in my long and sore exercises; but as I cast my care upon him, he hath cared for me; and blessed be his Name, he hath helped in my greatest straits, and hath made hard things easy, and what he shewed me by his pure Spirit of light for my encouragement, before I came forth, he hath brought to pass. Glory to his Name for ever, may all those say with my soul that love the leadings of the light of Jesus; for though it leads through tribulation, yet it brings the soul sweet consolation, and therefore worthy to be followed through the self-denial; for it is through the daily cross that we obtain the reward of the crown. And precious is the feeling of the life of Jesus to the awakened and illuminated soul, that made the roaring sea, and dry land, and lonesome wilderness all one to me by night and by day. Great was my encouragement to commit all that my Heavenly Father had given me, to his keeping, and to follow him, and in taking up the daily cross, I found power to preserve me from looking out at my affliction of body, when sorely exercised in mind, ready to sink under the oppression of it. Had not the Spirit of Truth, the Comforter, helped my infirmities, and taught me, I had never known how to pray as I ought; but I often read, That the prayers of the Lord's children avail much with him, and in these latter days, according to his promise, his are taught by him, and in righteousness they shall be established, and great shall be their peace. And this is the effect of our Heavenly Father's great unspeakable love to those that watch unto prayer, and continue in the same; for I know not how any can expect a child's portion, that breaks his Father's commands, and does not repent; and who is it but knows that watching and waiting is generally commanded? Surely it is a duty that ought to be performed by every one that is come to an understanding; and by believing in Jesus, the light and power of God, all may receive strength to perform it; and for want of understanding how nigh he was to me in years that are passed, I was long in a desolate condition, and could not be satisfied without acquaintance with the teachings of his Spirit, which is light. But I was then in darkness, and under the shadow of death, longing after the countenance of the Lord to shine upon my tabernacle; for if it should be dissolved, I was not sensible of a better building eternal in the heavens; though I read of them that had, yet I knew not their foundation; and whatsoever I builded, it came to loss, till I knew Christ Jesus, the rock and sure foundation of the heavenly building. And blessed be his Name, the inspiration of his Spirit is very precious, without which none can have a right understanding; and I could not find peace with God while I did err for want of this good understanding. And my cry was often to the Lord, to give me an understanding heart, that I might discern between things that differ; for the crooked serpent, who is very subtle in his workings, endeavours by flattery and threatenings, temptations, buffettings, and false accusations, to darken the heart, and enfeeble the mind; and if he cannot prevail so, he can transform himself into the likeness of an angel of light, to hinder the travailling ones, whose understandings begin to be opened, yet watching in the light, they come to see his snares; then he bestirs him, as a strong man armed indeed, as by experience much might be spoken, since I was first exercised about going this voyage. I shall omit as much as I can, having nothing in my view but Truth's prosperity, and preferring it above all, because it is better to me than all. I can do no less than bear my testimony unto all people, that its excellency far exceeds the choicest gold, and the precious pearls; and the Spirit of Truth comforts the comfortless, strengthens the weak, and relieves the needy. Oh what can be compared to its power! for it works a change of the heart, and preserves from sinning against the Lord, all those that follow the leadings of the light thereof unto amendment of life, and honour the Lord by ordering their conversation aright, according to the dictates of his Spirit. Oh, I had rather mourn away all my days than grieve it, or walk contrary to it, whatever reproach I suffer; for I have had a blessed reward when I have observed it, and obeyed it; and I hope I shall never forget how the power of it brought me into subjection, and made me willing to be disposed of by it. And when it had wrought me into a single resignment, then was my weighty concern (touching my journey to *New England*) taken off, and a service laid upon me to go back, and labour for the settlement of our women's meetings in our county of *Berks*, which was no small cross to take up. But as I daily followed Jesus, (honoured be his worthy Name,) he endowed me with his eternal encouraging power, and also strengthened the weak and hindermost of the flock. Though *Amalek* lay in wait by the way, and the opposite spirit did strongly strive, yet our good Shepherd did visit his handmaids, and (blessed be his Name) filled us with his overcoming power, when the mothers in *Israel* were so dismayed, as we were likely to have lost our women's meeting; but praises, honour, and renown, be ascribed unto that Almighty power that hath set up and settled this women's meeting, saith my soul; for it hath been a good reward to me, and fitly furnished me for the service that was required, and wonderfully upheld me therein unto admiration. I can truly say, my reward is sufficient, and can give in a true testimony, that the Lord owns our women's meetings; and hath manifested and magnified his excellent power therein, to the gladdening of our hearts, and the refreshing of our souls wherever I came. Glory to his Name, and magnified be his preserving power for ever. He is a God of wisdom unto the foolish, and strength unto the weak, and honours his power in contemptible vessels, that it may have its due; for all honour belongs thereunto: but those that are in the wisdom of the world, which comes from beneath, and have many arts and parts, and mind not the wisdom that comes from above, they take that to themselves which belongs to God, and that provokes him to wrath. He is angry with such as seek honour one of another, and do not seek his honour more than their own interest, and honour to man; for that hath been the overthrow of many. God is jealous of his glory, *he will not give it to another, nor his praise to graven images.* The secret arm of his power is stretched out to overturn them, and he is on his way, and it is in vain for *flesh to strive against him, before whom all nations are but as the drop of a bucket: for out of the mouths of babes and sucklings he will perfect his praise,* both in males and females that give up to serve him; and he brings great things to pass, contrary to man's wisdom or expectation, that *no flesh might glory in his presence.*

For when I was exercised about settling the women's meeting, I little thought to be concerned again with going to *New England;* but after a short time it was more weighty than ever, and my exercises more than before; and this I do write, that no one should murmur, and say, *No exercise is like mine.* And this followed me until the hand of the all-wise God was so heavy upon me, that I could no longer stay at home, although both sick and lame, and had much to undergo both inwardly and outwardly, yet did not dare to plead with the Lord any longer, or to make any excuse, but truly gave up all, both life and all that he had given me, when he required it; and he brought me to be *as clay in the hand of the potter.* He filled my vessel with his heavenly treasure, and fulfilled that scripture that testifies that he hath said, "*I honour them that honour me*"; and blessed be the Lord, such honour have the earthen vessels of a remnant, and the excellency of the power is his, and the glory of all; for he is worthy of it. He is no hard Master, but a sure Rewarder of his faithful servants, and he endues them with power that delight in his law, and incline to keep his commands, and unto such they are not grievous, but joyous; but looking out hinders; and therefore let none look at their own weakness. Let my harms make others beware, and let us be depending on our good Physician, for he hath the balm of *Gilead* that cures both soul and body, which makes the weak strong, with the sweet cordials of his life, that relieves the faint-hearted and feeble-minded, and through tender mercy I have found it very needful, and very useful at all times in all conditions; else what could I have done when in such a weak condition, so many thousands of miles from my habitation? But blessed be the Lord, and magnified be his preserving power, as trials did abound, patience did superabound, and that brought me to a good experience of that which sweetened my bitter cups, and that caused the living hope to spring, that anchors in stormy times. Then did the light of my soul's beloved shine upon me, and he shewed me what great deliverances he had wrought for me, and what great cause I had to trust in his Name, that had been a comfortable refuge unto me at home and abroad, and also shewed me, that his *rod and staff had comforted me;* and he was always with me, and in the enjoyment of his presence did my soul rejoice in the midst of great trials, and then was my cry, *Lord, give me and mine the comfortable enjoyment of thy presence for ever, and then try us as thou pleasest. Thy preserving power is all that I desire of thee, and unto it I commit all, and with thee I leave all, for thou art worthy to dispose of all; and then would life flow in as a river, to the comforting and strengthening of soul and body. Everlasting praises, and holy thanksgivings be returned to Christ Jesus, for he is worthy, my soul can truly say; for I have experienced his dealings, and seen his mighty works that he hath done, even marvellously for his tender seed, with which my soul hath travailled, and is often concerned; for they have much to bear wherever I have been.* The Lord my God relieve them more and more, and work their deliverance for thy own glory, and the comfort of thy true travailling ones for evermore.

Written on board the ship, in the
3rd month, Anno, 1681.

A FURTHER TESTIMONY FOR THE MAGNIFYING OF THAT POWER THAT SUPPORTED MY WEAK BODY, AND COMFORTED MY POOR SOUL IN MY TRAVELS IN AMERICA: I FEEL MYSELF CONCERNED TO GIVE A RELATION OF SOME PARTICULAR PLACES AND SERVICE.

FIRST I came to *New York*, and there had been hurt done by some, that Friends had lost their fifth-day meeting, and I laboured to settle it again, and God's eternal power wrought wonderfully in me in several meetings with his people, and we were well refreshed. And when the meeting aforesaid was settled again, it was with me to go to *Long Island*,

and there the *Ranters* oppressed *Friends,* but the Lord had a tender people there, and his power was amongst them, and we were sweetly refreshed together; for God's *almighty power was over all,* in all our meetings wherever I came, to the subduing of the dark power that raged in the *Ranters,* and the relieving of the tender hearted. Honour and praises be ascribed unto it for ever; for it made me sensible of the oppression of the tender seed, and for its sake my soul was in a deep travail; and the night before the General Meeting, I was near unto death, and many *Friends* were with me, who did not expect my life, and I was so weak when I came there, that two *women-friends* led me into the meeting. There was a great meeting of several sorts of people, and in a little time the God of wisdom, life and power, filled me with the Word of his power, and I stood up in the strength thereof, and it was so prevailing over the meeting, that *Friends* were very much comforted and refreshed, and the power of darkness so chained, that the opposing *Ranters* and *Apostates* could not shew their antic tricks, nor oppress *Friends,* as they used to do; for they were very abusive in those remote islands, and commonly did much mischief in *Friends'* meetings. And they that had been convinced, and were *turned again with the dog to his vomit,* as saith the scripture, and with the *sow that was washed, to wallow again in the mire, and had made shipwreck of faith and a good conscience,* they were most wicked. They preached scripture, and had Truth's words, but grieved Truth's spirit, and burdened *Friends* exceedingly, and honest *Friends* could hardly be clear, that had a testimony, except they spake while they were speaking. But when God's power did arise over them, it many times put them to silence, even to admiration; and although *Friends'* exercise was great, especially those that declared, yet the blessed effect of the Almighty power was, and is, a precious recompense, and a good reward.

And when my service was over in *Long Island*, it was in my heart to go to *Rhode Island*, to the General Meeting that approached soon after I arrived there; yet we had a quick passage, through providence; and when I came to the General Meeting of *Friends,* there was that abominable crew, and *Thomas Case,* the grand *Ranter,* was bawling very loud; and I had been there but a very little time, but God's living power did arise most wonderfully, and I declared in the demonstration thereof, and soon put him to silence; and he went forth, and the powerful presence of the Lord was amongst his people; and this General Meeting in *Rhode Island* lasted four days together, and I had good service there, and God's eternal heart-tendering power was over all, glory and living praises be unto it for evermore.

And still it was upon me to go to *Boston*; for that was with me before I came from home, and I hastened to take a passage in a sloop, and went with some *Friends*, and one was a *maiden Friend*, that had a few words sometimes in meetings, who had been there once before, and she and another *Friend* suffered much there, both imprisonment and other cruelty, for conscience sake. But blessed be the God of all our mercies, we had peaceable meetings there, and his excellent power was so, that it tendered the people, and there were hardly any that I saw, but shed tears; there was a *Lawyer* that had a hand in the suffering of our *Friends* that were put to death, and he was very solid all the while. And after this I travelled by sea and land in the strength of the supporting power to many places, whithersoever the Lord ordered me; and as I followed the line of his Divine Light, he failed not to endow me with the renewing of his precious power, and my soul hath cause to magnify it, because it enabled me to answer what the Lord required of me, and fitted me, who was the most unfit, and the poorest and most helpless that ever I did see concerned in such a service. But it was the more to the honour of the power of my God that so wonderfully wrought in my poor weak and helpless vessel; and many *Friends* were tendered thereby in many places, in the sense of my weakness. Honoured and renowned be it for over, saith my soul; for its manifestation made the hearts of his people glad, and we were well refreshed together in all the meetings that I was at in *New England.* And from thence I returned back to *Rhode Island* and *Long Island;* and when I was clear thereabouts, I took shipping for *East Jersey,* and the power of God was greatly manifested, and through his special providence we were preserved, being in great peril and danger of being cast away when we were in sight of land; for the winds being boisterous, and the foaming sea in so great a rage, that we could not cast anchor to stay the vessel, being near the shoals; but the Lord who hath all power in his hands, delivered us (praises to his holy Name), and we safely landed at *Shrewsbury. Elizabeth Dean,* who then travelled with me, was very sick. We had very good meetings in *East Jersey,* where I met with the Lord among his people, as at other times, blessed be his Name. After some time spent amongst them, in which we had been well refreshed with God's holy precious living power, it carried me from thence to *West Jersey,* and into some part of *Pennsylvania,* (but it had not that name then,) and in the sense of God's great love to his tender seed, I encouraged his children to suffer, and to be careful that they did not cause Truth to suffer; for if they tendered it in their own bosoms, and travailed with it, the Lord would bring it over all its enemies, and it shall reign over all in his due time. Blessed be his most worthy Name, he soon after brought it to pass by his delivering power; and when I had laboured that the gospel-life might be lived in, and the gospel-order established amongst them, there remained the heavenly power among the tender ones. And the Lord heard the cry of the poor, and granted the desire of the needy, and visited them with the gospel-power; for a little time after I came home, I had an account that they had men's meetings and women's meetings in the gospel-light, life and power, and were establishing in the blessed order that was testified of, when I was there with them.

And when I was clear of *West Jersey* and those parts, I returned to *New York*, in order to take my passage for *England;* but before I came there, the living God (whom I served with all my heart) further tried me, and laid it weightily upon me to go to *Barbadoes,* which was no little cross to my mind; but the overcoming power of the true and living God wrought so strongly with me, that I was made willing to take up the *cross, and follow Jesus,* through many tribulations, and he (magnified be his power) most wonderfully supported and conducted me all along. I took shipping at *New York,* and as the Lord put it into my heart to visit friends in the *Leeward Islands,* so he carried the vessel, let them that sailed do what they could; and they could not steer their course to *Barbadoes*, although they endeavoured with all their might. I had good service amongst them in the vessel, and they were made to confess to the Almighty power that I testified of. We lay off *Antigua* a week before the owner would let me go on shore, but the all-wise God ordered it so, that the vessel could not go away till I had been there, and performed what service he had appointed for me; and blessed be his Name, his reward was precious; for we came on shore on a first day, and I hastened to a friends' meeting; and when I came in, I found that the Lord's power was amongst his people, and I had a precious time with them. There was a little handful of plain-hearted friends, and our hearts were tendered, and our souls comforted, and we rejoiced that the Lord Jesus had visited us, and caused us in his love to visit each other.

So when I returned to the sea again, it came into my heart to visit friends at *Nevis;* and after I had taken leave of friends of *Antigua* who came on board with me, God's heavenly power which was with us, and had sweetly refreshed our souls whilst we were on board the vessel, remained with us, and we were concerned one for another, not knowing that we should ever see each other's faces more. But see how the Lord ordered it; as we were sailing on the sea, it opened in my heart to visit friends at *Nevis*, but the owner of the vessel being a hypocritical professor, caused my exercise to be the more; but the power of the Lord was manifest, and *the winds and sea obeyed*, that we were carried to *Nevis* against his will. But he would not let me go on shore, for he had heard, *That those should pay a great fine that carried any friend thither;* and hoisted sail again for *Barbadoes*, and said, he would weather the point of *Guadaloupe;* and he laboured three weeks, but could not do it: for the hand of the Lord was against him; else he might have done it in a few days, but he provoked the Lord, and trusted in his vessel, and in his own skill. He locked up the bread, and dealt hardly with his passengers, when he saw he should be longer at sea than at first he did expect. He knew that for three weeks there was stinking water, and we were close by a *French* island, and they said the *French* would not let us have any, if we starved. They were papists, and said, *If we came for water they would take our ship for a prey, and us for captives.* Yet this owner of the vessel would not go to any other island, until the merchants that were on board threatened him very sorely; and then he put in at a mountainous place, called *Mount Serat;* and they went all away from me as soon as they were landed; for I was very weakly, being on board the vessel so long, with such bad accommodation. I went on shore with my clothes so wet, that I could wring water out of them, and so dried them upon my weakly body, which cast me into such a feverish condition, that I was very dry, and I sat down on the shore, and a girl came to fetch fresh water near where I sat, and I drank till I sweat, and then I swooned, and lay some time; but the arising of the life of Jesus set me on my feet again, and in the strength and relief thereof I went to enquire for a passage for *Barbadoes*, and heard of none. But I was not clear of *Nevis*, and hearing of a leaking vessel to go to *Antigua*, took my passage in that, hoping that way might be made from thence to go to *Nevis*, and then having got a passage, it being night and rainy, I tried to get me a lodging on the land. The people were generally *Irish* papists, but the Lord did so order it, that I met with an *English* woman, and she treated me kindly, but she had neither bread nor drink, but wine and sugar; and I desired half a pint of *Madeira* wine to be boiled, and that served me night and morning, and the Lord blessed it to me, and his holy power accompanied me. While I stayed for the vessel, I had good service there, though there was no friend in all the island; they had banished a friend out of it, as I heard, but a little before, and the people told me they did not dare to have a meeting, yet I published Truth in the streets, and they confessed to it. And so I left Truth honourably amongst them, and then came on board the vessel, where I last took my passage, and sailed to the other vessel, that I had suffered in, and called for the owner and cleared my conscience to him, and told him the hand of the Lord was against him, and warned him to repent, else he should suddenly feel the stroke of it to be heavy upon him; and inasmuch as his heart had been too much set on that bark, he should shortly see that the Lord would destroy it, and accordingly his vessel was split on a rock in a little time after. So when I, through tender mercy, came to *Antigua* again, the friends told me how they had been concerned for me, and so had *Nevis* friends, and there was a passage ready for *Nevis*, and an honest woman-friend, whose name was *Mary Humphery*, was very ready to go with me, and friends there were very joyful of my coming, and we had many good and powerful meetings in that island; and there was a judge and his wife came to meeting, and people of several sorts, and we had some meetings at the houses of them that were not friends, and friends were well satisfied and comforted, and the mighty power of God was with us. Glory unto it, for it is worthy over all, and in us all. Oh that we may have an eye to its glory in our whole lives and conversations; for it is by it we live, move, and have our being; and its dealing with us, and working for us in that place is worthy to be remembered; for this was the place that the owner of the vessel aforementioned was afraid to carry me to; but the Lord was on my side, and prevented much evil when it was intended; and the governor of that place was so kind that he gave us his letter of recommendation to carry with us. I came back with *Mary Humphery* to *Antigua* and to *Five Islands*, and there we and some friends that went with us visited a poor people that complained of their priest, and said he came to them but once a year, and then it was to take that which they had from them; and we had a precious opportunity to manifest the truth, and they were very kind to us, and seemed to be well satisfied and affected.

And then I being clear, and a passage presented for *Barbadoes*, as soon as I was ready I went on board, and was there sooner than could have been expected. And when I arrived, I met with many friends at *Bridgetown*, and there took an account of the monthly meetings, and went to them and other meetings as brief as I could; and most days I had two or three meetings in a day, both among the blacks, and also among the white people. And the power of the Lord Jesus was mightily manifested, so that my soul was often melted therewith, even in the meetings of the *Negroes*, or blacks, as well as among friends. And when I had gone through the island, and was clear, having been well refreshed with friends, in the feeling of the heavenly power; and in the strength of the same I came on board the ship for my native land again.

J. V.

Written on board the ship
coming from *Barbadoes*,
in the 3rd month, 1681.

BEFORE I went to sea I was two weeks in the service of Truth in *Kent*, and then it was shewed me, being at *Sandwich*, that I should bear my testimony for God, and his divine spiritual worship, in a *steeple-house* there; and coming home, the heavenly power wrought mightily in my heart. And when I was clear of those countries, I was better in health than I had been for many years. And as the light of Jesus shewed me, before I left *England*, as is afore hinted; so the power thereof ordered me when I came back, and it was so weightily on me before I came on shore, that I thought it long ere I came to *Kent* to clear my conscience. And the God of sea and land brought me safely thither, and I hastened to *Sandwich*, and on a first-day, being the 5th of the 4th month, 1681, I went to the *steeple-house,* as it was before me, and had been of a long time, and in the strength of the Almighty power, I delivered that message which I received of the Lord Jesus, saying *The day is come, spoken of and foretold by the Prophet, of the pouring forth of God's Spirit upon all flesh, sons and daughters, etc.* And I exhorted them, both priest and people, to take heed to a measure or manifestation thereof in their own hearts, (and leave off their idolatry) and come to be true spiritual worshippers; and I laid before them the danger of the one, and the benefit of the other; till the priest caused me to be haled out; and when I came forth many of his hearers followed me, and I had a good opportunity with them, and cleared myself to them, and left them. And as I was going away, I felt the arising of that power that is worthy to be obeyed, and it was with me to go to them again; and when they came from their worship I met them, first the mayor and his company, then the lawyer and his, and after that the priest, with many more. I invited all to come to our spiritual worship, and I would engage that if any of them, young or old, male or female, had a message from the Lord to deliver there, that they should have liberty, and not be abused, as the priest caused me to be; for the man that haled me out hurt my arm, so that it was swelled some time after. I told the priest that he was not of the primitive faith and Church of Christ, testified of in scripture; for there, if any thing was revealed to the standers by or hearers, they might speak one by one, the first holding his peace; and he was silent before I spoke, and he said I should not have spoken in the Church; and I asked him what Church that was? for I had spoken in the true Church many times amongst God's people, and they did not hinder me; and he said *Paul* spoke against a woman's speaking in the Church. I asked him what woman that was, and what Church that was that she should not speak in? And he did not answer me, but went away; and a woman-friend that was with me took hold of him, and said, "my friend, answer the woman's question," (and the *Dutch* people were coming from their worship the while,) but the priest put off his hat to us and bustled away, and afterwards endeavoured to send me to prison; but the God of power (who preserved me when much evil hath been intended) prevented him, that he could not prevail with the mayor, but he endeavoured to harm the friends of that place after that I was gone. And after the first-day meeting was over, I went at the beginning of the week to some other meetings, and came again on fourth-day, and God's power was over all, and friends had no harm; and we had another heavenly meeting, and so I came away and left friends peaceable, and all was well, blessed be the Lord, and magnified be his preserving power, over all, for evermore. *Amen, saith my soul.*

J. V.

I was informed that the priest above specified, did do his endeavour to stir up persecution against friends, and put the mayor to some trouble, for not punishing me; but therein he did, nor could do, no more than manifest his own malice, and what birth he was of: the Lord had set his bounds.

J. V.

In this long journey, this I can say, (to the honour and glory of my tender God, and to the praise of his providential power,) and be it known to all, that although I had none to accompany me of my own or friends' providing, yet the Lord so ordered it, that I had still some honest woman, or maiden friend, both by sea and land. In the first vessel that ever I was in, I had an honest ancient maiden friend, named *Sarah Yoklet,* who was my companion from *London* until I came to *Long-Island.* And then in *New-England,* one *Lydia Wright,* another faithful friend, was willing to travel with me, and did accompany me a considerable time; and still the Lord so ordered it, that whenever one left me, another was ready to take her place to be my companion; and when I returned home, there came with me an ancient maiden friend, who had been out in those countries in the service of Truth six years, whose name was *Margaret Kerby.* On the 3rd of the 4th month, 1681, I arrived safely at *Dover,* in the county of *Kent,* where I was three weeks in the service of Truth; and after that (blessed and renowned be the holy Name of Jesus) I came to *London,* and after a little time spent in visiting friends in *London,* I came safe home. And as I pondered weightily, and beheld the preservation of me and mine, and the manifold mercies that we received when so far remote one from another, my heart was truly tendered in the sense of my heavenly Father's love, and my soul magnified the preserving and delivering power, and the cry ran through me, *Lord God of my life, let me and mine never forget thy goodness, for it is wonderfully to be admired; and thy inexpressible love to be considered, by all those unto whom it hath been so largely extended. And as I consider our nothingness, and thy tenderness towards us, I cannot but abhor self, and breathe unto thee, that I and mine may for ever hold self in no reputation, and follow Jesus through the daily cross; wherein I (through tender mercy) have found power, when of myself I could do nothing whereby to fulfil what was required of me, but self was very ready to hinder me, as the self-seeking spirit always is to hinder those that are not aware of it. And therefore I desire, above all things, that I and mine, whom the Lord hath been so good unto, may be watchful; and, in order thereunto, I commit all unto that God of power that hath preserved hitherto, and is able to keep and preserve unto the end. To whom be all glory and praise for evermore.* Amen.

J. V.

A LETTER WRITTEN AT GRAVESEND TO FRIENDS OF THE WOMEN'S MEETING, BY J. V. WHEN SHE WAS GOING TO SEA, FOR HER LONG JOURNEY.

DEAR and well-beloved sisters, my love and life salutes you; even in a sense of the tender love of my Heavenly Father do I embrace you, and greatly encourage you to keep your women's meetings, and keep up your testimonies, every one in your places; for every one hath a testimony for the pure God, though not in words, yet in the Word of life, which hath quickened our souls, and powerfully operated thereon, even in our women's meeting. Hath not the sense of it been sufficient to engage our hearts to serve him; and to bear our faithful testimony for him in purity of life and conversation, that his Name may be honoured, and the precious Truth propagated? For this you know how long hath been the travail of my soul amongst you; and, I hope, it will be the travail of yours in my absence, that if ever we see one another's faces again, it may be with joy and not with sorrow. So let your breathings be for my welfare in the Lord Jesus, as mine are for you; for had it not been to keep covenant with my God, I could not have given up my weak body to the sea; but in my long and sore exercises, I often promised the pure God, that I would give up my life as a sacrifice, if he would accept of it; and now he hath tried me, and if he please to take it, it is but my reasonable service to offer it up to him. I did intend you should have had more timely knowledge of it, but that I could not tell whether it might have been taken from me; therefore I forbore speaking of it publicly, till at length I could not longer refrain; but now, in the universal love of God, do I take my leave of you all, not knowing whether I may see you again or not. Remember my dear love to the brethren, whose labour of love and work of faith is for the propagating of the precious truth.

And the Lord God eternal keep us all close unto

himself, in that which neither sea nor land can separate; for in it my love doth truly reach unto you all, being clear in the sight of my God of all service, save only this which my life lies engaged for. Here I stand resigned to live or die in the will of my God, and so I desire him to keep me to the end.

And, dear friends, be valiant for the Truth, that it may not be undervalued through a cowardly, creeping, libertine spirit, for that hath done too much hurt already; stand over it, I beseech you all, and quit yourselves like faithful soldiers, fighting under the banner of love, which our tender God hath spread over us, that we may not be ashamed to bear the cross; and take heed, lest any cause the offence of the cross to cease, for such are enemies to Christ Jesus, let them profess what they will; for there is no way to the Crown, but by and through the Cross. So, in that which brings us into subjection, do I remain (present with you in spirit, though absent in body) your tender sister in the precious Truth.

J. V.

From *Gravesend*, the 24th of the
12th month, 1679.

Let this be read in your Women's Meeting, or anywhere, as a service is seen.

A LETTER TO HER HUSBAND, RICHARD VOKINS, SENT FROM RHODE ISLAND.

DEAR HUSBAND, my love and life salutes thee, with my dear children, and my father, and my brother *O. S.* and his wife, and my brother *D.* and his wife, and all the rest of my dear friends and heavenly relations, dearly desiring your preservation and prosperity in the ever blessed Truth; and then I doubt not but our God will increase us in our outward store. And, dear heart, thou art often in my mind, and the breathing of my life is for thee, as for my own soul, and I do believe that all our trials will work for good, if we love the Lord Jesus as we ought to do. Those trials that we have had, and do now meet with, I hope will fit us for greater, and I do not know but I may come home again to suffer with you, by the strength of the same Power that hath preserved us hitherto. Oh, magnified be it for ever, saith my soul, for it hath done for me great things. And, dear heart, my service is greater here than it was there, and I have pretty well cleared myself in *Long Island,* but at *New York* I am not quite clear, but I hope I shall ere long. I am now at *Rhode Island,* going on to clear myself as fast as I may, as the Lord makes way for me. I intend to take the meetings between this and *Boston,* and when I am clear there, I hope you may hear further from me, or see me, in some reasonable time, as our tender God shall be pleased to order. And by this you may all know that my tender God is with me, and carries me through many sore exercises, and his mighty power enables me to do his service; and his reward is not wanting, blessed be his Name, for all his tender mercies. Friends are tender to me, and I am better in health at present than I have been; but I have many ailments attending my weak body still.

So, dear heart, let us breathe to our God together, though outwardly far asunder, yet if it stands with the will of our Heavenly Father we may see one another again, to his honour and our comfort; and let us pray unto him, day and night, that we may be content, to be at his disposal in life or death, together or asunder, that he may be honoured, and our souls comforted.

And, dear heart, remember to have an eye over our dear children, that they lose not the sense of truth, which my soul hath so deeply travailed for, when I was with them; for it is my fear, now I am from them, that if thou do not supply my place in my absence, that the spirit of this world will prevail and hinder the work of the Lord in their hearts, and in thine too, and that will be to all our sorrow. The Lord God eternal keep us faithful to him unto the end, that we bear our testimonies for his Truth with boldness at all times, and in all places, that we may not be ashamed to confess him before men if we should come to be tried for our lives; for it is a precious advancement to be a worthy sufferer. And if the mighty God do bring me home again, to partake of suffering in my native land, I hope those exercises that I now go through will still fit me for greater; and I hope this is the end for which thou and I am tried. And so, in the love of that which is able to preserve us, do I once more salute thee, and remain,

Thy true and tender wife,

J. V.

From *Rhode Island*, the 14th of the 4th month, 1680.

REMEMBER my dear love to my children, and bid them mind the Lord, and to all friends of our meeting, and let my son *R.* tell them that I greatly desire their faithfulness, and I hope he will have an honest testimony for God. I would have *Mary* see this letter, that she may be of a believing heart, that if the Lord should bring us together again, it may be to his honour, and our great comfort; the Lord is as well able to preserve me home, as he was hither, and I hope he will in his time, I must leave that to him, and so I hope will you; for if we be not contented with his will, it will not be well with us. And, therefore, let us learn *Paul's* lesson, for we have great need in every state to be content. No more, but dear love, being in haste,

J. V.

TO OLIVER SANSOM AND HIS WIFE.

DEAR BROTHER AND SISTER, whom I dearly love in the Lord Jesus, (our life,) who makes hard things easy, bitter things sweet, and bears up in the greatest trials, do I salute you, with my *Mary*, my sister *Margery*, and the rest of them, earnestly desiring your prosperity every way, as of my own soul. And by this you may know, that though sore exercises and travails attend on every hand; yet I am alive to magnify that Power that hath preserved in dangers great, and difficulties many, and is able to preserve unto the end, and therefore I desire that we may trust in it, and obey it, to the honour of it; for it hath been manifest in my weak body, to the admiration of many of the upright in heart, and they are very loving to me wherever I come. And my tender Father hath strengthened me to do his service in *Long Island*, and *New York*, and in

Rhode Island, and *Boston*, and *New Jersey*, and those parts of *America*, and I was in hope to have come home when I was clear of *New England;* but the Lord hath laid it upon me to go to *Barbadoes*, and in his strength I am going thither in a vessel, of which one George Fletcher *is the owner and master, who professes Truth.* Do you not think that a line from you would be very precious to me? I have neither heard from, nor seen one of my native land since I left it; but I cannot blame you, not knowing whither to send or direct a letter. Remember my dear love to all friends of our men's and women's meetings, earnestly desiring their faithfulness therein, and in all things else that pertain to the life of Truth, that we may bear our testimonies in uprightness unto the end, that in the end God may be glorified, and our souls comforted, for ever and evermore. Dear *Anne Lawrence's* children are in my mind as well as my own. I hope you will look after them in my absence, that we may have comfort of their growth in the Truth, if ever we are present again; and if they grow in the Truth, and knowledge, and love of God, then will the desire of your tender sister be answered. And so in that which satisfies our breathings, I remain,

Your tender sister,

J. V.

The 1st of the 8th month, 1680.

FOR FRIENDS AT GRAVESEND, IN LONG ISLAND, AND ELSEWHERE.

DEAR FRIENDS, my love and life salutes you, and in that which unites unto our God and endears us in the heavenly relation, you are often in my remembrance; and my soul's desire is that we may feel each other in a living growth, in that life and love of God which reaches over sea and land, and satisfies our souls, and causes us to rejoice together in spirit, as present (though absent in body) joining in the God of our sweet salvation. Though in this world we meet with many bitter exercises, yet blessed be his holy Name, his sweet salvation outbalances all; and as in the Light we behold it, we have great cause to magnify that Name that bringeth it; for there is power to make the weak strong, and to establish the feeble-minded; and we have sufficiently partaken of its preservation and deliverance. Glory and honour and praises over all be returned thereunto, our souls have cause to say, for all his mercies and great loving-kindness, both spiritual and temporal; for his wonted favours and renewings of mercy daily. Who can consider it, and not be bowed into tenderness before him? The consideration thereof melts my heart even at this time. And the breathing of my soul is to the God of my life, that we may all keep low in the valley of our Father's love, where the well-spring of life doth overflow; that our souls through its sweet refreshings may live unto him, that through its arising we may magnify his Name and celebrate his praises, for death and darkness cannot. And therefore we had need be all watching in the Light, and waiting for the arisings of Life, that death and darkness may be subdued out of our families, and out of our assemblies; that our families may be seasoned with the heart-cleansing and preserving holy fear, that they may be of God's families, and our assemblies crowned with Life; that Truth may be promoted thereby in our generation, and our posterity blessed in the generations to come. For this end the Lord hath taken compassion on us, and raised us up of all the families of the earth; and if we do not answer the requirings of his love, he may lay us by, and raise up whom he pleases.

Oh! dear hearts, feel his love, for it requires love my soul can truly say. Oh! what manner of love is this (as one said in his day) that he hath loved us with, that when we were afar off and strangers to him, he made known his precious Truth unto us, and revealed a measure thereof in us, to help our infirmities and to teach us, when we could find no comfort in all the teachings of the idol shepherds, nor no help for our infirmities. Oh, how precious was his voice, and comely was his countenance, and how tenderly were our hearts affected therewith, in the day of our convincement! Oh, it was a day of love never to be forgotten! And how hath he surrounded us by his power ever since? Surely his Fatherly love hath been and is sufficient to oblige us to obedience; for he is not wanting to his tender seed, but is appearing for the affliction of *Joseph*, to work deliverance for *Jacob*, and to relieve the travailing seed, in the remote corners of the earth. There are many going and gone out of *Old England* to *Pennsylvania* and *New Jersey*, that have been as instruments in the hand of the Lord for the promoting his Truth here; and I hope they will be so there, to the honour of his great Name and the comfort of his children in the neighbouring *Islands;* for the Lord will exalt his Truth, though the wicked grow worse and worse.

Therefore, let our hearts magnify his Name, and our souls (and all that is within us) return praises and thanksgiving unto him, for he is worthy, who is God blessed for ever, and evermore. *Amen*, saith my soul, who am a travailer in spirit for the tender Seed, and a rejoicer in its prosperity.

JOAN VOKINS.

This Epistle, it is supposed,
  was written soon after
  her return home.

Let this Epistle be copied and sent to *Matinicoke*, to *M. Pryer* and friends thereaway, to be read among them.

Here follows the copies of some more Letters that she wrote and sent when she was in AMERICA.

TO HER HUSBAND AND CHILDREN.

DEAR HUSBAND AND CHILDREN, my endeared love, in the love of my tender God, doth dearly salute you, and the breathing of my soul is unto my tender God, that you may be faithful and obedient to your measures received, that you may grow in the knowledge and love of God, and of his Son Christ Jesus, *whom to know is eternal life*, which is better than natural life, or any thing that thereunto belongeth. Oh, dear hearts, consider of it, and forget not the goodness of the Lord; for unutterable is his love towards us. My heart is tendered in the feeling of it, and I cannot forget his tender dealing with us; and the cry runs often through me to the God of my life, that you may not forget his goodness, nor slight his tender love, nor neglect your duties to him; for, dear hearts, he is not a hard Master, but his reward is sufficient to engage our hearts to his service. Therefore let our hearts be encouraged to continue in well-doing, and to watch against the enemy, that he may not prevail to draw out your minds from waiting upon the Lord. Surely there is great danger attending you, my dear and tender ones. Oh, let your hearts be diligent to seek the honour of God, and the exaltation of his Truth, above all things; then I shall have the desire of my soul answered. For I am greatly concerned for you, and my prayers are for you night and day, that your souls may live to God, whatever your bodies endure. But for your comfort, I put you in mind of the sweet promises of him that said, "*First seek the kingdom of heaven, and the righteousness thereof, and all things else shall be added.*" And I am truly satisfied, he is never failing to fulfil his sweet promises unto them that *keep his commandments;* and if we love him, let it be manifest by our keeping his commands; for *he is worthy to be feared,* and trusted in, and depended upon, and had in remembrance continually. *The Lord God of my life stay your minds, that you may wait upon him, that in his own time, and upon his own terms, you may partake of the fulfilling of his sweet promises, which are attained unto by loving the Light, and living the life of Truth.*

And so, dear hearts, let us be singly resigned unto our God; for I can truly say, his love is most deeply of an engaging nature; for by it I have been preserved from great dangers, perils by sea, and perils by land, and perils amongst false brethren; but out of them all his mighty power delivered me, and I am yet alive to magnify it, glory, and honour, and everlasting praises be unto his Name for evermore, saith my soul; for he daily filleth my heart therewith, and makes me able to do his service beyond expectation; and he is not wanting to communicate to my soul, (glory to his worthy Name,) but his reward is in my bosom, which gladdens my heart, and refreshes my soul, and upholds my weak body, that I am not without hopes of seeing you again; for I have cause to say, *There is nothing impossible unto my God*. I have been most of this winter upon the roaring seas, two months at a time, and saw no land, and my clothes were not off two nights all that time, so far as I can remember, and there was no conveniency for my weak body. There were *French*, and *Dutch*, and *Irish*, and *Barbarians*, and *English*, and I had sore exercises amongst them, both inwardly and outwardly; but yet I had good service also amongst them, and they did confess to the power of my God; although they were most of them very wicked, yet they were chained by it, and the passengers were kind to me for the Truth's sake. When it pleased the Lord to bring us to land, we arrived at the island of *Antigua*, in the *West Indies;* there I found a precious people, and had two meetings a day for a week, with white people and blacks; on the seventh day is their children's meetings; they have also men's and women's meetings, and the gospel order is established and establishing in those remote islands. Glory to God for ever! They teach their children *G. F's.* catechism. We went on board the ship again, designing for *Barbadoes;* but our small vessel was so heavily laden, that we could not get from the *West Indies,* but kept up and down another month, so that the passengers were all weary; and the water grew scarce and stinking, and I was very weak. When we came to another island, we who were passengers were willing to go on shore, but the vessel did not enter there; my exercise then was very great, for I had great drawings to go there, and the weight of my service remained with me. A few days after we bore up, and went to another island, where there were no friends, and there I went on shore, with some of the other passengers, but I knew no person there. The inhabitants were most part *Irish,* and I was almost spent when I came there; but the Lord was exceeding good, and comforted me every way, and I got a passage back again to *Antigua;* and it remained with me to go to the island of *Nevis;* for I could not be clear of the weight of it. When I had been sweetly refreshed, through the love of my God, amongst them again at *Antigua,* way was made for me to go from thence to *Nevis,* and an honest widow went along with me, who was very helpful to me. We had good service amongst the blacks and whites. She remembers her love to you all, and her prayers are with mine unto the Lord for you. Now we are clear of *Nevis*, and going again to *Antigua*, I hope the Lord will make way for me to be at *Barbadoes* ere long, for I understand it is but a week's sail, or two at most, if the wind sits fair. When we came from *New York*, they spoke of but three or four weeks' voyage to *Barbadoes*, and we came out thence about the time called *Michaelmas*, and I have not seen it yet. I sent you many letters from thence when I came away, by which you may know my service in *New England*, and the time when I came away from thence. I do not know whether you received any of my letters, but I have taken all opportunities I could, both by sea and land, to send. I met with a vessel upon the sea the last letter that I sent, and she was bound for *London*. I do long to hear of your welfare, but I do not blame you that I receive no lines, except you could tell whither to direct them. I have not seen one of my native land, that I knew, since I came forth. But the Lord is with me, and unto his preserving power I commit you, with myself, and all the tender ones, that *Amalek's* spirit may not hurt the hinder part of the flock, nor turn the weak out of the way.

Dear hearts, let us be single unto God, that our understandings may be opened, and kept open, that no subtle spirit may betray our innocency. And let us never forget the watch; and if we fulful that command, God will be honoured, and our souls comforted for ever and for ever, and for evermore. Forget not your family meeting on first-days at evening; let not any thing hinder.

J. V.

Written in the Island of
Nevis, the 11th of the
11th month, 1680.

And in the same Letter there were a few lines added to her son, Thomas Vokins, *being then an apprentice with* William Gibson, *in* London.

Dear Son, T. V., my love salutes thee, and thy dear master and mistress, and all the faithful in Christ Jesus, earnestly desiring your welfare as my own. And, dear heart, let thy honest endeavours answer the desires of my heart; for my soul's breathing is, that thou mayst be kept low and chaste; that thou mayst fear at all times; that thou mayst do as *Joseph* did, who could not sin against his God. Oh, dear son, it is a precious thing to feel the awe of the Lord upon thy heart. Oh, that this may be thy state; that thou mayst be found watching unto prayer, and continue in the same; that thou mayst witness preservation from all the enemy's snares; and that thy mind may be stayed in the light, to wait for the incomes of life; that thou mayst live to God, and seek his kingdom, *and the righteousness thereof*, and then thou needst not fear but *all things else will be added.* I hope thy diligence and faithfulness to God, and unto thy master and mistress, will increase their love to thee. So hoping thou wilt take good counsel, and bring forth the fruit thereof, to the honour of our precious God, and to all our comforts.

This is from thy tender mother,

J. V.

AN EPISTLE TO FRIENDS OF NEW YORK, AND THEREAWAY.

DEAR AND WELL-BELOVED FRIENDS, these lines are left to your weighty consideration in this season, whilst opportunity doth present, for times and seasons are in our Father's hand, and we know not how soon he may put a period to our days; and, therefore, we are all concerned to seek the propagation of the precious Truth, whose excellency far exceeds the purest gold, and the gain thereof far transcendeth all earthly treasure. Oh, let it be our greatest care to be affected with it, that we may say with the apostle, in a living sense thereof, that *godliness with contentment is the greatest gain;* for we might well know, that no other gain is profitable for our everlasting welfare. Neither will anything else stand us in stead when God calls for an account of our talents; and, therefore, let it be the bent of our hearts, and the inclination of our minds, to improve them, that we may give our account with joy; that our God may be honoured, and our souls comforted when this momentary pilgrimage shall be ended, and all our troubles and exercises forgotten. The fulness of that which we have already the earnest of, being an hundredfold better than anything we have parted with for it. And if we should be yet tried to part with all, even life itself, it is but our reasonable service to give it up to him from whom we have received it. For what have we (that is good) but what we have received of him, and what is it that he is not worthy of? Is not his love sufficient to engage our hearts to his service? Has he not delivered us in dangers deep, and difficulties great, and brought us through many and sore distresses? And hath he not made us partakers of many precious promises? Endless praises be to his most holy Name, saith my soul. The feeling of his sweet refreshing life that he communicates to my soul, is a hundredfold better than husband and children, or any outward mercies that he hath made me partaker of, though very near and dear unto me. And now, dear friends, the scriptures are fulfilling in us; therefore let our earnest that we have received, engage our hearts to our Master's work, that we may receive the fulness of that which we already have an earnest of, for we have not a hard Master to serve; but, behold, he comes, and his reward is with him. Oh, let us wait for him to enlarge our hearts more and more, then shall we love to propagate his Truth, and run the way of his commandments with joy and great delight, that we may all witness the fulfilling of that sweet promise of a hundredfold in this life, and afterwards the great and double reward of the faithful, which is the joy of the soul in the life which is everlasting.

And so, dear friends, let us all keep a narrow watch over our hearts, that the spirit of this world do not creep in, to draw the mind from that which did at first convince us; for that is as precious as ever, and never waxes old, and, therefore, let our zeal for it never wax cold. Let us prize all opportunities to assemble together, that we may feel our hearts inclined, singly to wait, that we may receive a further dispensation of life, that a growing people we may be; that love unto our God, and unto one another may abound amongst us; that the way of our God may not seem unpleasant, nor his commands grievous unto any of us. Neither that giving way unto which would lead into the liberty of the flesh again, for that is a dividing spirit, that will separate from God, and uncement and break the unity of the body: it is of a creeping nature, and enmity lodges in it, whatever it may pretend; and because it hath already wrought in a mystery, and brought dishonour to the worthy Name of our God, and reproach upon the precious Truth. Therefore it doth deeply concern us to double our diligence in doing our duties to honour him, in the propagating of the Truth.

Oh, friends, let us for ever have this before the view of our minds; let no other beloved hinder; for if we love anything more than this, it will not go well with us; for our God will search the camp, and if there be a *Babylonish* garment, or a wedge of never so precious gold, yet if the work of the Lord be hindered thereby, his wrath will surely come upon it and consume it; for a clean camp the Lord will make, that his Truth may be renowned. The day of purifying is come and coming more, in which the hypocrites shall be tried, and the upright in heart comforted, although there may be many that were first, come to be last, and some, *Judas*-like, betray their Master; yet the Lord will spread his Truth in the nations, and magnify his own power, by staining the glory of all flesh, and by laying self low before him, that it may be had in no reputation. He will not give his glory unto another, the adulterer, nor the idolater shall not be decked with his jewels; for where self is decked, the Lord is provoked; but where self is denied, and the daily cross taken up, there the low appearance of the Son of God is bowed unto, which seems contemptible unto them, who cause the offence of the cross to cease, and settle upon their lees, and sit down in a state of carelessness, thinking themselves secure, without the performance of their duty, in obedience to the measure of Truth received, that should bring into a disciple's state. Oh, friends, we all know, that rest is polluted, let us all up and be doing, that our lamps may be trimmed, and we all may be ready to meet the bridegroom of our souls, that we may enter in while the door is open; but if we delay until the door is shut, then it will be in vain to seek, we shall not be able to enter, when the door is shut against us; then what will the profession of Truth do for us.

Therefore, let us with one heart and mind labour together, and let our breathings be one for another, that the possession of life may be more and more inherited amongst us, that we may be refreshed one in another, when together or asunder, that sympathizing one with another, we may, as members of one body, to the honour of Christ our holy Head, from whom we receive nourishment, to keep us from withering, grow and be useful all in our measures, that one cannot say unto another, I have no need of thee; for if we are cemented together as members of one body, we must needs be all concerned for the honour of our Head, and the comfort of one another.

I remain, your unfeigned friend in the precious unchangeable Truth,

JOAN VOKINS.

Written in the Island of *Antigua*, in the movings of the Spirit of Truth, and in the sense which that gave me of the state of friends there.

This to be read amongst Friends at *New York*, (or elsewhere,) as in the wisdom of God it may be seen meet.

Here follows a Letter that she wrote on board the first vessel going for AMERICA; *directed, and sent to some women Friends in* LONDON.

DEAR FRIENDS, I cannot forget your labour of love, and sisterly care concerning me, and do return the acknowledgment thereof, with kind acceptance.

This is to certify you, that after I left *Old England*, I had no cause of doubt or fear; but the roaring sea is to me as the dry land, because of my Heavenly Father's presence and power, which makes hard things easy, and bitter things sweet, in whose arms we have been preserved hitherto, and we have great cause to hope we shall unto the end; for he is with us, and has done for me already, more than I did expect from his tender hand. I have not had one fit since I came on board; but *Sarah* and I are both sea-sick. We have good encouragement in our voyage. Here are some friends, and some other sober people, and I have good service amongst them; and the peace of my God flows in as a river, and his love and life as a mighty stream, which I would not be separated from, for all that is in *Old England*. Let all friends know, that ask concerning me, that it is very well with my soul. Glory everlasting be unto my tender God for ever! Though my body is weak, yet he that made it, is worthy to have the disposing of it, and unto him it is resigned, for he hath often brought it down, and raised it up, and can do with it as he pleases.

And let my dear husband and friends thereaway know, that I am at home with my God; though absent from my outward; and he that clothes the lilies, and feeds the ravens, takes care of me as well here, as at home; and as to my bodily weakness, I am not worse than I was at home, but much easier in my mind. Blessed and magnified be the Name of the Lord for ever.

It is troublesome for me to write, the vessel doth so wave. I desire that *Susan Dew,* and *Mary Elson* may see this, or have a copy of it; also, my dear husband and children, to whom my endeared love is recommended, and to all our friends thereaway, that love the Truth, and walk in it; for they can sympathize with me, and are partakers of the reward of life with me in our own bosoms, which is, and hath been more to me, since I have been on board the vessel, than my natural life. It is the best cordial that I can ever have, for healing virtue is in it, by which my soul and weak body are strengthened and comforted in times of great weakness, sore trials and exercises, in the sense of which my soul is tendered before the God of my life; not questioning but that we may see one another's faces again with joy, and not with sorrow. And if we do not see face to face, yet if we abide together in spirit in the work and service of our God, then shall he be honoured, and our souls comforted, and so shall I have the desire of my soul answered, who am a travailer for the tender Seed's sake, in the service of Truth, wherein I greet you all in the salutation of my dear love, and therein do take my leave, and bid you farewell in the Lord Jesus, remaining,

> Your true and unfeigned friend and sister
> in the precious Truth,
>
> J. V.

From on ship-board in
the *Downs*, 27th of the
12th month, 1679.

AN EPISTLE TO FRIENDS IN RHODE ISLAND,
AND THEREAWAY.

DEAR FRIENDS, my love and life salutes you all that love the precious Truth, and live in it; for they are very dear and near one unto another, even as epistles written in one another's hearts that cannot be forgotten; not written with ink and pen, but with the uniting and healing Spirit, that unites us unto our God, and endears us one unto another, in which I am one with you in trials and exercises. The breathing of my soul is unto the God of our lives that all may be cut off that trouble you, and that the love and life, and all other spiritual graces and gifts may be multiplied and increased in and amongst you, that you may persevere as the worthies of the Lord, that through renewings of the right spirit you may be more and more conquerors over all that is wrong; for our God is on his way. Glory to his Name for ever! He hath regard to the very hindermost of the flock; therefore, let all put on valour and courage to follow the Lamb, for he is on his way triumphantly. He and his faithful followers shall have the victory, though we may meet with much by the way, yet we have great encouragement still to look to him who has hitherto preserved in dangers deep and difficult; and though in this world we meet with many troubles, yet our Helper is nigh, yea, a God at hand to deliver out of them all. Surely his love is sufficient to engage our hearts to his service; for we have every one a service for our tender God in our places, and purity of life and conversation is that which will answer to the establishing and confirming of all that keep thereunto. Though the outward appearance of things may make some weak ones to reason and question, and be ready to stumble, yet the gospel light and life, and the good order thereof is very comfortable, and as it is kept unto will resolve all doubts, stop the dark reasoner, and put a period to all unprofitable controversies, which things the Lord grant may be brought to pass amongst you, and in all the churches, to the honour and exaltation of his holy Name and precious Truth, and the comforting, building up and establishing of every breathing tender babe, that he over all may have the praise, and our souls the comfort for evermore. *Amen*, saith your friend in the unchangeable Truth.

J. V.

From *Barbadoes*, 6th of the
1st month, 1681.

Let this be read among Friends in *Rhode Island*, as the wisdom of God shall direct.

Here is at the *West India Islands* a very good precedent concerning children, and I could wish that it were so among the Lord's people everywhere. Friends' children meet together once a week, and sit together with their parents, and wait upon the Lord, and are instructed, and they learn dear *G. F's.* catechism* at home, [*and then they say it at the meeting once a week*] and I do believe that it does produce a good effect; I can truly say, that the power of the Almighty is amongst them, for many of them were tendered and shed tears when I was at their meeting, and friends were refreshed.

Here in *Barbadoes* are family meetings very frequently and comfortable.

---

* This probably refers to a work published by George Fox, in 1657, entitled, "A Catechism for Children, that they may come to learn of Christ the Light, the Truth, the Way that leads to the Father, the God of all Truth."

AN EPISTLE TO FRIENDS IN EAST JERSEY.

Dear Friends, be of believing hearts, and keep to the measure of Light already received, that none may be veiled in their understandings, and so come to loss; but that all may have the benefit of their own measures, that we may magnify our God together; for in the feeling of that spirit that helpeth our infirmities and teaches us, we are greatly encouraged to travel on, though there is much to be met with by the way. Oh, therefore, let none be weary in well-doing, but all be diligent, that God's plantation may flourish in every heart, that he may have the fruit to his glory, for he is making manifest his great love to his tender Seed in those remote corners of the earth; and he will make his Power known, and his gospel light is shining, and he will multiply his mercies, and increase his blessings, both spiritually and temporally, unto those who live the gospel life, and keep to its blessed order. Oh, the great love and tender dealings of our God, that he is visiting those islands, which causes my soul often to rejoice; for he has heard the cry of the poor, and is arisen for the help of the needy, and has made many willing to leave their native land, that are as instruments in his hand, for to build up in the pure victorious faith, which has long been the breathing of my soul for you. For the Seed's sake I have been concerned closely with the God of my life, and the cry in me hath often been unto him to send forth more faithful labourers amongst you, that his vineyard may be dressed and cleansed from all that hindereth its growth, and he hath heard, and answered in measure, blessed be his Name. Oh, friends, let every one be concerned, and none be idle, but all to the work of the day, lest night come and prevent you.

For now is the day-spring from on high visiting you, and the affliction of *Joseph*, and the troubles of *Jacob*, the Lord has removed, and for his Seed's sake will yet more appear and work its deliverance in the hearts of all that are truly tender of it; although the serpent is very subtle and busy, and always trying to betray innocency; yet the watch being kept, he is prevented, and our souls preserved. Therefore, dear friends, let us not forget that command, lest the enemy should prevail. Oh, feel a necessity of watchfulness, that we may keep our hearts diligently; that we may feel the issues of life; that the inward man may grow and be capable to act for God; for we have every one, both male and female, a service in our proper places; and they that are diligent in doing their duty, shall be sure of a blessed reward of life and peace; therefore, let all be encouraged that are poor and needy, and feeble-minded. Oh, let them put on courage, yea, the very hindermost of the flock; for our Captain is courageous, he goes on conquering and to conquer victoriously, and by his power he brings great things to pass, and is working deliverance for his suffering Seed, that hath breathed to him in secret, and could not be satisfied, but was without all hope of help, until the ancient power was brought to light, and the spirit of Truth revealed, to help our infirmities, and to teach us to depart from iniquity, and to do the things that are well pleasing unto our God. Oh, the day of our convincement! in which our hearts and souls were tendered, and we made sensible of our states, is never to be forgotten; but the ancient power that tendered us then, is to be kept unto, that we may do the work of the day; for the gospel day calls for purity of life to adorn it. Oh, that we may be, as *John* said, fearing God, and giving glory to him, for the hour of his judgment is come; and we and ours ought to fear him, and stand in his awe, and not sin against him. Oh, that we above all things may endeavour that our families may be of his family, and our assemblies crowned with life, that living sacrifices may be offered in our spiritual worship; for broken hearts, and contrite spirits, our tender God will never despise.

And, therefore, dear friends, let us keep low in the valley of our Father's love, where the wellsprings of life do flow, that a living people we may be, to the praise of our God, and the promoting of Truth in generations to come; that our offspring may be encouraged by our good examples, successively to honour Truth when we are gone to our rest; that our posterity may be blessed of the Lord, and be to his praise, and our everlasting comfort for ever and for evermore. *Amen.*

Written in *Barbadoes* in the
1st month, 1681.

AN EPISTLE TO SOME FRIENDS IN NEW ENGLAND, BUT IT HATH RESPECT TO THE GENERAL STATE OF FRIENDS THERE.

T. AND ANN POTTER, dear friends, my love doth truly reach to you and your children, desiring your welfare every way, even as for my own, not forgetting your love to me when I was there, but in a sense of that love that our God hath shed abroad in our hearts, do I salute you, earnestly desiring that our children may be his children, and that they and we may magnify his power together, though outwardly far asunder. Oh, that we and ours may truly endeavour after this; for it is the breathing of my soul that we may feel one another in harmless hearts, that we may breathe one for another, and be refreshed one in another, though absent in body, yet present in spirit, serving our God, and eyeing him that he may direct our hearts, and keep our minds stayed, that when the winds do blow, and the storms do beat, we may be upon a sure foundation. For all foundations shall be tried, and the sandy buildings will not stand in the trying times; and, therefore, we had need be builders up of one another in our most holy faith, that we may be firmly established, and as good soldiers enduring hardships unto the end. For our Captain is on his way, glory to his worthy Name! He goes on triumphantly conquering, and to conquer, and he and his faithful followers shall have the victory, and his love is sufficient to encourage the feeble ones, for by his power we have been preserved in dangers many, and very great and difficult. He hath been a present help in the times of our greatest need, and though we have in our travail here, met with many troubles, yet he (who is our God at hand) delivers out of all. Everlasting praises be unto his Name for ever! He hath made known the spiritual armour. Oh, that we may rightly prove it, that the strongholds of sin and satan may be pulled down, and righteousness and holiness set up in the place thereof, that our God may be honoured, and his Truth exalted, and his children comforted for ever, and for evermore. *Amen.*

Mind my dear love to *Elizabeth Hooten*, and to the friend and her husband, (that went with me to *West Jersey*,) and to *William Asten* and his wife, and *Thomas Leeds* and his wife, and let them know that I should be glad to hear that a meeting was settled at *Middleton*. Mind my love to *S. Cooper*, and his wife and family, and let them and other friends know, that I believe there would be great service in establishing a meeting there. My love to *R. Lippingcot, William Shaddock*, and the friend *Warner*, and to all the rest of friends; for my love is truly to them all, as if I named them and their wives one by one.

And my fervent desire is, that the precious Truth may prosper amongst you; and that faith and patience and love and life, and all other spiritual graces and gifts, may abound amongst you; and that all that is wrong may be purged out. Oh, that all of you would wait to feel the renewings of the right spirit, that there might be no room in the heart, to entertain the wrong spirit, to hinder or hurt innocency. And the Lord God of my life discover its subtilty, and keep us all upon our watch, that none of us may be taken in his snares, for they are many and dangerous: and therefore I commit you with myself, and all that love the Truth, and live in it, to the never-failing God, who is worthy to be feared and obeyed, trusted in, and depended upon by us, and all that love him, for ever and for evermore.

You would say, that I have great cause so to declare, if you did but know what he has brought me through, since I left you: but blessed be his Name; he enabled me to do his service everywhere; and friends are kind and loving to me here at *Barbadoes*, and so they were at the *Leeward Islands*. No more, but unfeigned love; and rest.

Your friend and sister in the precious Truth,

JOAN VOKINS.

From *Barbadoes*, 14th of the
1st month, 1681.

TO FRIENDS IN **WEST JERSEY.**

DEAR FRIEND, *William Peachee*, after the salutation of my love to thee and thy wife, and friends, this is to let thee and friends there know, that I cannot forget you; but the travail of my soul is for you; and the tender God of my life has heard the cry of his oppressed Seed, and arisen and will appear more and more for its deliverance. Although the *Philistine* spirit doth strongly strive, and *Amaleck* lay by the way, yet *Israel* is greatly encouraged and hath great cause to travel on, for the Captain of our Salvation, is going on before us conquering and to conquer. He will gather his sons from far, and his daughters from the ends of the earth; for this end he visits the dark corners, and for his Seed's sake he has appeared on your behalf. If you mind the gospel light, and live the gospel life, and keep the gospel order, then will God's plantation grow, and bring forth fruit to his praise, and then you may expect his blessings and prosperity upon you and yours. But if you slight the great love of God, and let in the spirit of this world, and get you other lovers, that will greatly provoke the Lord, cause him to withhold his mercies from you, and cause you to fail of your expectations. This loving caution sprang in my heart unto you, and in that which thinks no evil I leave it with you, hoping that in the same you will receive it, that in the reading, our lives may be refreshed together, though in person far asunder. For it is exceeding precious to me, and my life rejoices at the feeling of a living brother or sister's growth in the Truth, and it is what my soul travails for, who am a friend to it; and as I feed with you in the land of the living, we can sing together as the ransomed of the Lord; and the breathing of my soul is, that all that are there may be preserved, and that many thousands more may be gathered to the honour of his great and worthy Name and our mutual comfort, for ever and for evermore. *Amen.*

J. V.

From *Barbadoes*, 1st month, 1681.

A SHORT TESTIMONY AGAINST THAT SPIRIT OF DIVISION, THAT GAVE FORTH W. R.'s BOOK, STYLED, "THE CHRISTIAN QUAKER DISTINGUISHED."

WHEREAS there is a libertine spirit at work, very busy, to darken the hearts of them that touch with it: I feel a necessity upon me, and that from the Lord, to bear my testimony against it; and to caution all the tender ones not to meddle with it, lest they be tinctured and hurt by it; for it is a subtle spirit, and seeks, under fair pretences, to betray innocency, and some there are that are come to a loss thereby, as woful experience doth daily show. Therefore let it be considered, how it is with those that are alive to God; and how it is with those that are within the bounds of that spirit, which gave forth *W. R.'s* wicked book, and those that own it, are they not in a dying condition, as to the pure life of Jesus? And let them whose understandings are not clear, take heed how they read in it, lest they bring a veil over them again they know not how. I may say, from a certain sense, that it is a dark spirit, and too many are groping therein; and that is the cause they do not see wherein the difference lies. Oh, that every such a one would keep to that which did at first convince them, that they might have their understandings opened, and kept open, that they might see how far they are on their spiritual journey, that this self-seeking spirit might not betray in the wilderness; for there are howling deserts, and dangerous places, where this spirit hath lurking corners, and creeps in at every turn, if the watch be not duly kept! And therefore let all take heed and beware of this destroying spirit, whatever it does pretend, it is no better than the inwardly ravening wolf, though clothed outwardly like a sheep, and therefore deceives the more. The Lord will lay it open more and more for his own Seed's sake, that has long suffered, and the upright hearted, who are true to God, shall have great encouragement to travel on; but those that are looking out are in great danger of being ensnared by this spirit, which may make their journey long and tedious, by muddlement of mind, and sometimes go backwords, yet their way may be so hedged up that they cannot get quite back to *Egypt* again, but may die in the wilderness, if they take not heed Oh, that all, while they have time, may come into obedience to the Truth, and feed together in the land of the living, that in the feeling of life we may sing together as the ransomed of the Lord, dwelling with him, out of all strife, in purity of life, cemented together in the bonds of his love, with our affections fixed on things above!

J. V.

TO FRIENDS IN **NEW ENGLAND**, AND THEREAWAY.

DEAR FRIEND, SAMUEL SPICER, my love salutes thee and thy dear wife, and father and mother *Tilton*, if yet alive, and the rest of friends of your meeting; and friends at *New York*, earnestly desire your welfare in the Lord Jesus, and breathe to the God of my life, that above all things Truth may prosper amongst you, and that faith, and love, and peace, and life may be multiplied amongst you, that the work of the day may go on, whatever you meet with to hinder. Though the *Philistine* spirit doth strive, and *Amaleck* lie by the way, yet good encouragement have we, as faithful soldiers enduring hardships, to travel on and follow our Captain fully; for his reward is sure, though it is through many trials obtained. Yet when this momentary pilgrimage is passed through, the greater weight of glory will out-balance all; and in the sense of it, let our hearts rejoice, and our souls magnify that power that has preserved, and is able to preserve unto the end; and that in and through it we may be strong in the Lord Jesus, fitly furnished to every good work, and that we may never be weary of well-doing, nor faint in our minds. Though in this world we meet with many troubles, yet we know him that is able to deliver out of them all; and if he feed with the bread of affliction, and the water of adversity, yet blessed be his living Name, he teacheth our souls to profit thereby. And we have cause to say in this trying day, as the three children did in ages past, We know that our God is able to deliver us, if he please; but if he will not, we will still trust in him; for he has been with us in six troubles, and we have good cause to depend upon him, and to have confidence in him in the seventh. For it is but a little while and persecution and affliction shall come to an end; but the word of patience, that preserves in times of great temptation, abides for ever, and shall never have an end. Glory, and honour, and living praises be returned and ascribed unto the God of all our mercies and blessings, both spiritual and temporal, which we daily partake of from his fatherly hand; for he is a never-failing God, and of his loving-kindness there is no end! And unto the protection of his almighty power, which reaches over sea and land, do I commit you, with my own soul, henceforth and for evermore.

Your sister in the unchangeable precious Truth,

JOAN VOKINS.

From *London*, the 3rd of the
1st month, 1682.

TO FRIENDS OF **CRANBROOK, IN KENT.**

Dear Friends, my love salutes you, and the rest of the faithful in Christ Jesus, who hold fast their integrity and retain their first love; for such are near and dear unto me, and often in my remembrance, whatever exercises they undergo; and my soul doth often breathe unto the God of my life, that we may be kept in a waiting frame, that if trials and afflictions do abound, that his sanctifying Power may superabound, that as faithful soldiers, we may endure hardships to the end; that in the end we may receive the greater weight of glory, that may outbalance all the momentary afflictions that we meet with in this short pilgrimage. Oh, glory to his Name! who is the physician of value, that can cure both body and soul; he is worthy to be trusted in, who never fails them whose confidence is in him, and all things are possible for his Power to do; therefore let our dependence be on it for ever, that we may feel it in all our undertakings, that we may have the benefit of it in the use of the creatures, that his blessing may be upon them, then it will go well with us, whatever may come. That the Lord Jesus brings to pass, for the honour of his own worthy Name, and the comfort of our weak bodies, and everlasting benefit of our immortal souls, is the desire of

Your true friend in the unchangeable Truth,

J. V.

4th of the 9th month, 1682.

FOR THE FRIENDS OF ABINGDON MEETING, IN BERKSHIRE.

MY DEAR AND WELL-BELOVED FRIENDS, if you will be delivered, then keep to Truth, and that will set you free from sin, and from iniquity; and if you would wear the everlasting crown, think not for to sit down at ease, but follow the Lamb through the many tribulations, that you may partake of his sweet consolations; for the more trials and sore exercises do abound, the more the love and life of Jesus will superabound unto all them that do believe in him, and suffer with him, they shall assuredly reign with him, and be crowned with life, that are faithful unto death; and what is left upon record we see fulfilling, that all that will live godly in Christ Jesus must suffer, and the worst enemies are those of their own house. Let them read that have experience, for they may understand me, and such I truly sympathize with, in the patience and suffering of the Lamb, knowing that he and his followers are deeply engaged in the spiritual warfare; and truly it is a precious and a blessed cause to be concerned in; and them that love any thing more than him, are not worthy to be concerned in his war, neither can such partake of his government and peace, which shall never have an end.

Therefore we that go this spiritual warfare, must not be entangled, but must follow our Captain through the many tribulations; bearing our faithful testimonies, that our garments may be made white, being washed in the blood of the Lamb; that the precious adorning of his meek and quiet spirit we may be covered with; that we may feel justification by him in our own hearts; then we need not fear what man can do unto us. Though all men should rise up against us, yet if our God be for us, he can take our part, and plead our cause, and soon subdue our enemies, if he pleases. But if he will not so do; yet we have cause to do as the three children did, to trust in him, however; for he knows what is most convenient for us, and he will cause all things to work together for our good; and if he gives the bread of adversity, and the water of affliction, yet, glory be to his worthy Name! he teaches us to profit thereby, and what he orders for us is still for the best. Let us wait to feel his sanctifying power to strengthen us to follow him, which way soever he leads; that we may love him above all perishing things, and manifest our love by keeping his commands. One of his commands which he gave unto all his, is to watch, to be aware of their soul's enemy, and to enjoy the sweet benefit of their soul's friend, which far exceeds the friendship of all the world, and for the same we can turn our backs on the glory of the world, and do choose rather to suffer with the Lamb and his followers, than to enjoy the pleasures of sin for a season; for that would captivate our souls. Though we might have more favour from the wicked, and more ease to our bodies, but if hardship be our portion, and that we must have a sufficient share therein, yet our reward is sure, if we endure to the end. Glory, and honour, and praises unto the God of all our mercies, and that for evermore! His blessed everlasting reward will out-balance all; therefore great encouragement have we to wait upon the Lord Jesus. for the renewing of our inward man, that we may continue in well-doing, those few days we have to spend in this momentary pilgrimage, that in the end God may be glorified, and our souls, after all trials and sore exercises are ended, may be everlastingly comforted.

DEAR FRIENDS, by this you may see that I do not forget you, though so weakly in body, that I cannot visit you; yet am with you in spirit, and as long as we abide in the precious Truth, the Spirit of Truth writes us, as epistles in one another's hearts, that cannot be forgotten; and in the same I dearly salute you, and bid you farewell in the Lord Jesus. Though in this world you have many besetments, yet under his tender compassionate care I commit our cause, and unto the protection of his almighty power do I commend you, with my own soul, henceforth and for evermore.

Your sister in the heavenly relation,

J. V.

Chawlow, 1st of the
6th month, 1683.

CONCERNING HER JOURNEY INTO IRELAND.

DEAR FRIENDS, by this the blessed Truth, and they that love it may be cleared, that have unity with me in my service; for I have a witness in every heart, that I may appeal unto. But those that take no heed to the Spirit of God, the true witness in their own hearts, can have no experience of the work of it in others, and, therefore, no marvel if they wonder and perish, as said the apostle, though they say daily, and weekly, and year after year, it is their duty to love, and fear, and obey God with all their hearts, with all their souls, and with all their strength; yet so far are they from the doing of it, that they are ready to cast aspersions on those that do. And though it is written in the Liturgy of the Church of *England,* that it is their duty, yet they will not wait upon Jesus to receive power to perform their duties; and, therefore, they abide in unbelief and disobedience, not considering their time is short, and the work of sanctification is great. Oh, how dangerous a thing will it be, to have such a weighty work to do, when there is no time to do it! Well said the apostle, *"Work out your own salvation with fear and trembling;"* was that the way then; and is it become ridiculous now, that so many are so much averse to it? Oh, where are the mockers and scoffers, and persecutors of our age? Who are hearing and reading the scriptures without understanding. Oh, that they would take heed to that which reproves for evil! that their understandings might be opened by it; for that is the spirit that the holy men were inspired with, that gave forth the scriptures; and until the hearts of people be turned to it, their understandings are so darkened, that they cannot see the state of their own souls; much less understand the holy scriptures. Therefore we need not care what such can say or do against us, who truly fear the Lord, for our reward is from him; and we have good cause to serve him, and seek to exalt his blessed Truth, by preferring it above all things. Though relations may be near and dear, yet to part with them, and natural life and all, is but my reasonable service, if my God requires it; for I have found him a bountiful Master, and no respecter of persons. Those that truly fear him, and work righteousness, do find acceptance with him; and that is more to a remnant, than to find acceptance with all the potentates of the world; for their favour will not procure peace with God; neither can those live in God's holy heart-cleansing fear, that offend him to please man. In vain will it be for any to hope to die in favour with God, and not live so in his fear, as not to offend him; and notwithstanding all the talk of loving the Lord Jesus, and fearing him, yet there are none do it, but those that leave off doing evil, and learn to do well; and such keep his holy commands, which are not grievous, but joyous to them, when the Lord doth enlarge their hearts, then can they run the way of his commands with great delight. But while man or woman standeth at a distance from that good Spirit that God hath, in his tender love, given them to profit withal; they cannot be sensible of the Lord's enlarging their hearts, nor of his working in them, both to will and to do of his own good pleasure; therefore, let all have regard to the work of God's holy Spirit in their own hearts, that they may come to be sensible of the goodness of the Lord, and the mighty works that he doeth for their souls; and from a living experience invite others to come and taste and see for themselves, how good our God is. For of a truth he is good unto his *Israel*, that are of an upright heart in his sight; and they can say of a truth, That one day in his courts is better than a thousand years in kings' palaces, and in the presence of the Lord is the fulness of our soul's joy; and at his right hand are durable riches and pleasures for evermore; and, indeed, it is weighty to consider, how many are preferring the honour of man, before the honour of God, and earthly riches before the heavenly treasure. And how eagerly do mankind press after outward gain, and slightly esteem the gain of godliness, though, with content, it is the greatest gain of all.

But, my dear friends, you that can do nothing against the Truth but for the Truth, I leave these lines with you, that the weak may not be turned out of the way, nor the feeble caused to stumble by any false aspersion, that the devil, through his instruments, may be permitted to cast upon me for the Truth's sake. For I have given no just cause to any to speak evil of me; but if any should take occasion to speak evil of the precious Truth, because of my serving it, let them know, that for this cause it was made known unto me, that I might truly serve it and not myself; and if they that are carnally minded would do so, they would then indeed know, that to be carnally minded is death, but to be spiritually minded is life, and peace, and true contentment. And this I write as one that has had a woful experience of the enmity that lodges in the carnal mind, and a good experience and privilege that redounds to the souls of the spiritually minded, and do earnestly desire that those who are carnal and sold under sin, as the apostle said, may turn unto that which is to slay the enmity; for it is nigh unto every one. It is the word of the Lord which is the sword of his Spirit, and as a hammer to break down the partition-wall of sin, which separates the soul from the presence of the Lord; and it must be known so to be, before men can be fit to receive the things of God. Thus may people come to see between things that differ, and not call good evil, and evil good, and put darkness for light, and light for darkness, as too many do, by which the Lord hath been and is greatly provoked, his precious Truth vilified, and his children daily reproached as evil doers, and that by all sorts and sects. It is now, as it was in the days past, among the twelve disciples there was one *Judas*, but he did not defile the rest, but he went to the high-priests and rulers, and so sided with them, that loved not the appearance of Jesus. And so do these now, that love not his spiritual appearance, and can no more understand the work of his power in his children, than they could that said, they were *Abraham's* seed, when Christ told them plainly, that they were of their father the devil, and his works they were doing, though they were very high in the world's esteem, (at that time,) and he very low in theirs. He told them the truth, and they hated him; and we have read what became of them, and of *Judas*, when he could not find repentance, though he sought for it. O, therefore, let the harms of those, make all the disobedient and gainsayers beware in time, and seek to honour God by their subjection to the spirit of Christ Jesus, who is come to save his people from their sins, by his spiritual appearance in their hearts, that their souls may have the heavenly sentence pronounced at last by the righteous Judge, Well done, good and faithful servants, enter into the joy which is prepared for all them that believe in Christ, and suffer with him, while on the stage of this world, for theirs is the blessed reward in the world that is to come; and they that suffer with him here, shall reign with him for ever. And in a living sense of his almighty Power, that hath already been manifested, is my heart encouraged to go on in his service, not looking at weakness, or any outward thing that might by natural reason hinder; for who so poor, who so simple, who so weak, who so unworthy as I? Surely the Lord God of love is manifesting his almighty Power in contemptible vessels, that it may be the more magnified. Let all that take up the daily cross, and follow Jesus, magnify his power, for unto such it is daily manifested, to supply all their needs, and thereunto do I commit all, for ever, and evermore. *Amen.*

J. V.

Written by one that breathes for the prosperity of *Sion,* and desires the welfare of all people, 27th of the 5th month, 1686.

TO FRIENDS IN ANTIGUA AND NEVIS ISLANDS, IN THE WEST INDIES.

DEAR FRIENDS in the heavenly relation, which is nearer than that of blood, in which the God of all our mercies keep us near unto himself, and one unto another, that as he renews his mercies, we may renew our obedience unto him, and our love one to another, that while we remain here we may breathe one for another, that we may be refreshed together, though outwardly far asunder; that as children of one Father we may feed together at one table, and be nourished with the feast of fat things, which our heavenly Father hath provided for his sincere ones, unto whom his love hath been so largely extended, as to preserve in dangers deep, and made his wonders known, even unto a poor despised remnant, that he hath daily provided for. Glory to his worthy Name! and magnified be that almighty Power, that hath been so largely manifested in all our troubles, and helped us when we could not help ourselves, and had none to help. Oh, how hath it wrought deliverances many, unexpectedly! Surely we have cause to trust in it, and to depend upon it; for I have cause to say to the honour of it, there is nothing too hard for it to do! I have proved it, and seen its mighty works to admiration, and it is daily marvellous in my eye; for it is strength in the midst of my great weakness, a present help in times of my great need, and in the blessed enjoyment thereof I am sweetly encouraged to go on in my place of service, though in much weakness of body and outward affliction. By this you may know, that since friends' sufferings in *England* ceased, there was way made for my coming to *Ireland*. I had come sooner, but sufferings were so great, that I could not leave friends while it was so. As soon as ever friends came out of prisons, and before I could get strength after my long weakness, I set out for *Ireland;* but lest I should not live to come, I came forth in great weakness, because it remained with me to visit this land, and I have had a good experience of the tender dealing of the righteous God, who never required me to do any thing, but he gave me of his never-failing Power to perform it. In the strength thereof I travel on in my heavenly progress, wherein the Lord God of all our comforts and consolations preserve us all unto the end, whatever we have yet to meet with; that nothing may be able to separate us from the enjoyment of our heavenly Father's love, nor the seasonedness of his heart-cleansing fear, nor the refreshings of his daily supplies of soul-nourishing life, and supporting power, but, through the feeling of the same, we may renew our watchfulness, and faithfulness, and continuation in well-doing, for he is a never-failing God, and from him all good proceeds, and therefore, worthy to be waited upon all the days of our appointed time. Praises to the Name of Jesus, we have good cause to wait, and not to be weary; for certain it is that he accepts of sincere waiting, he renews the inward strength of them that truly wait, and diligently observe the dictates of the right spirit, and join not with any thing that is wrong; these receive ability to do that which is right in the sight of God, and in and through Christ Jesus, such come to partake of the daily renewings of life; whereby the heads of a remnant have been borne up in great trials, and sore and various exercises. Glory and honour be unto our God, through his son Christ Jesus our Saviour, for he hath saved us when much evil hath been intended against us, and hath filled our cups, and caused them to overflow! Praised, and honoured, and renowned be his holy Name, for it is worthy, and that for evermore! *Amen.*

J. V.

Written in *Ireland,*
  7th month, 1686.

TO THE WOMEN'S MEETINGS IN THE VALE OF
WHITE HORSE, IN BERKS.

DEAR and well-beloved sisters, whom I cannot forget, but in that love that reacheth over sea and land, does my soul dearly salute you, hoping that the pure mind will be stirred up in every one of you, to consider the matchless mercies of our tender God, which I do here put you in remembrance of. Oh, how hath he manifested his almighty power when we have been together in our women's meetings, and how have we been relieved and borne up over all opposition, both inwardly and outwardly, and in the gospel light have seen the great goodness of the Lord, and with the gospel power been strengthened when we were very weak, and supported when we were very needy? Hath not our heavenly Father's love been sufficient to engage our hearts to faithfulness? Oh, that it may be as an obligation to every one of us, to keep to the gospel light, and to live the gospel life, and to love the gospel order, for our God is a God of order. He affords precious opportunities to wait upon him, and if we abide in a good sense of his love, we shall not forget our times and hours to wait for the seasons of the Lord; for they are so sweet to the thirsty soul, that it cannot be satisfied without them, and therefore many times thinks it long ere the meeting day come, that it might be replenished with the virtue of Christ Jesus the Head, and strengthened with the rest of the members; for as we truly gather in his Name, (praises thereunto,) he hath made us partakers of his divine nature. Oh, how hath he bedewed our souls, and caused our cups to overflow, when the arisings of his eternal power hath been felt among us to rebuke the enemy, and keep him back, that would have hindered us from serving the precious Truth, and prevented us of the privilege of our women's meetings. Oh, that we may now take heed that we give him no advantage, by slighting the mercies of our tender God, or neglecting of our duties, but that in the remembrance of his tender mercies and Fatherly love we may double our diligence in our places of service, that our God may be honoured, feared, and obeyed by us all, that we may receive the blessed and sure reward in the end, when time here as to us shall be no more, and be in safety from all harm for ever, and for evermore! So be it, saith the soul of your dear sister in that which is strength to the weak, and help to the helpless, that sea nor land cannot separate.

JOAN VOKINS.

From the County of *Wexford*,
  in *Ireland*, the 26th of the
  7th month, 1686.

POSTSCRIPT.

So, dear hearts, by this you may know that my tender God is still exceedingly good unto me, and manifests his great power, and it is admirable in my eyes, that I am yet alive, to tell of his wondrous works. But blessed be his worthy Name, he preserves me by his almighty Power, and in his tender love provides for me! Since I gave up all, he is more to me than all. Glory to his Name, and magnified be his preserving and delivering power; my soul hath every day cause to say, for he hath done great and wonderful things for my soul and weak body, else I had not been alive at this day; but still am I an object of his tender pity, and do hope so I shall be the remainder of my little time a monument to his praise! Many sensible friends here are tendered in the sense of God's love when they see me travel in so much weakness. I hope that you and I shall praise his Name together, and magnify his eternal Power, though in person far asunder, for it is worthy to be magnified, as it hath been manifested; for if that had failed, we had failed; but because that lives, our souls live to speak well of the Name of our God, who is above all gods, and there is none like unto him: it is honour to us sufficient to serve him, for his reward is sure, and blessed be his worthy Name, he makes me a partaker daily of the gain of godliness with contentment, which is a continual feast!

Your sister in my measure,

J. V.

TO HER CHILDREN.

AFTER my dear love to my husband, this is to signify my tender love to the precious Truth, by my motherly care for my children, that whether I live or die, you may be careful and take heed that you do not stain the testimony of Truth, that you have received, by wearing of needless things, and following the world's fashions, in your clothing and attire, but remember how I have bred you up. Consider what manner of persons you ought to be, now you are come to years of understanding, that you may not grieve the Spirit of the Lord, nor me, nor any of his dear children. But that you may walk as becomes the gospel of our Lord Jesus Christ, that you may be good examples to others, and patterns of plainness and uprightness in your conversations among all people; then will the blessing of the Lord attend you, and it will be well with you in this world, and in that which is to come; then shall God be honoured, and my soul with yours, and with the souls of all his tender ones that desire the same be comforted, and Truth promoted over all; and then you will have cause to say with me, that its excellency far transcends all that the world can afford, and will endure when that shall pass away. And, therefore, forget not the spirit of it in your hearts, but take good heed unto it at your down-lying, and at your up-rising, that you with me may have the benefit of that promise of the Lord, who said, *He would be with his children at their down-lying, and commune with them at their up-rising.* And in this the day of his great love, he is nigh unto his children, and delights in them that abide in a watching and a waiting frame, and take counsel of his divine Spirit: *But woe unto them, that take counsel, but not of me, saith the righteous God, and cover with a covering, but not of my Spirit.* And, dear hearts, the day is come that all false coverings will be found too short and too narrow, to hide from the wrath of the Almighty, and they that are truly the children of the Lord shall be covered under the wing of his eternal Power, from the jaw of the strong destroyer. Though he may cast in floods of temptations, and may try by subtilty to betray innocency, yet, dear hearts, look not at that, lest your faith should fail, but look unto the almighty power of God, and wait to receive it, and believe in it, and keep to the measure already received, that will make way for you to escape the temptations, when you cannot help yourselves, and have no other to depend upon. Oh, then, how has he appeared for me, and manifested his preserving and delivering power! Oh, let your souls with mine, magnify it, for it is worthy, and that for evermore!

Truth is the same here as in *England*, and friends do not suffer the world's fashions to be followed, for both men and women here do go plain in their apparel, according to Truth, in a comely manner. The women do not attire their heads, setting their clothes aloft, imitating the world's fashions, wearing any needless things, nor in a needless manner. And some public friends from hence, are going to *England* in the service of Truth, and more to go, and they will be grieved to see friends' children stain the Truth, by attiring themselves not in modest apparel, and it would also be a great grief to me, if my children should be some of them. And, therefore, look to it, I charge you, in God's holy fear, that you may be warned and escape the dangers that do attend youth, and be preserved out of all the snares of the evil one, for they are many. And by this you may see, that I do remember you; and the breathing of my soul is daily for you, and for all my relations; and to them at *Farringdon*, and *Charney*, and *Goosey*, and all the rest of friends thereabouts. Mind my love to them all as opportunity is, and let them know, that the Lord God of my life, and the length of my days, is still exceeding good unto me, and enables me by his power to do his service; and blessed be his holy Name, his precious reward is with me, and that causes my soul to rejoice, and makes my heart more glad, than the greatest increase of all outward things! Oh, that it may be so with you, that your delight may be to serve him, according to your measures, that you may clearly see, by the bright shining of the Light, the vanity and folly of needless things in apparel, and that to lean after the world's vain unsettled fashions, is so far from being comely, or an ornament to any professing Truth, that it is great cause of shame for any such to be ensnared thereby! I am certain, that if you keep to the gift of Christ's Spirit, that is given you to teach you to profit, and to lead you into all Truth and plainness, I say, that I am sure that if you hearken to the Spirit of Christ in your own hearts, that then these needless things afore-named, and foolish fashions of the world will become a burden to you, as they are to me, and then you would be soon weary of them, and of all that is needless: round attire upon the head, set up aloft, &c. I desire, that the Lord may lay it home to your consideration. And you may also hereby know, that I have had not one well day nor night since I came here; but I am not worse than I was at home. I have travelled three hundred miles and upwards in this nation of *Ireland,* and am now going for the *north.* I have been often very like for death, but have not lain by it yet, blessed be the Lord!

I am uncertain when I shall be clear to return, but I intend to go no further than I have a necessity, because of the weakness of my body, and the winter drawing on, it is hard for me to travel; but the Lord is exceeding good unto me, beyond what I am able to express. My dear love to all relations and friends. I rest

Your dear mother,

J. V.

From *Dublin,* the 18th of the
9th month, 1686.

AN EPISTLE TO FRIENDS.

Dear Friends, in the covenant of life, whom the Lord in his unspeakable love hath done so bountifully by, as to reveal his Son in us, visiting our souls when in a lost condition, and could find no comfort. Oh, let his mercies never be forgotten, and the consideration of his tender dealing abide with us; and let the renewings of his tender mercies, both spiritual and temporal, give us fresh occasions to renew our obedience; for if we abide in the consideration of his love, we cannot but be tendered in the sense of the same, and brought thereby into true subjection to the sanctifying power, by which we have been and are preserved, notwithstanding all the dangers that hath or do attend. Oh, the excellency of the Power! it is so precious unto a remnant, that we have continual cause to glorify our Heavenly Father, with all, and over all, for he is worthy; and if it be with life and all, it is but our reasonable service; and those that will save that alive that is to die, do thereby deprive themselves of life eternal; and, therefore, we have all need to dwell low in the self-denying spirit, and the daily cross, that we may still enjoy the convincing power, that we may travel on in our heavenly progress with valour and courage, those few days that are to come, in which we may expect many troubles. But living praises to the God of our lives and length of our days, in Him we find that peace, that man cannot give nor take from us; and in Christ Jesus, our life is hid from all that are in darkness, and under the shadow of death; and because the Son of God lives, our souls live to praise his worthy renowned Name! His eternal power that has been manifested to tender our hearts, and to bring us into subjection to so good a Master, daily nourishes and enriches our souls with the reward of life in our bosoms, which causes us to say with the prophet, *One day in his courts is better than a thousand elsewhere.* And surely it is better to be a door-keeper in the house of God, than to dwell in the chiefest palaces of the wicked. Oh, how goodly are the tents of *Jacob*, where we find safety in times of need! As we abide in covenant with *Jacob's* God, we have cause to rejoice as *Israel* did, when the Rock that followed them was Christ Jesus, the Rock of Ages, the sure Foundation of the faithful, the hiding-place, as the shadow of a mighty rock in a weary land, to shelter the weary travellers by the way; the streams of *Shiloh*, that run so sweetly to comfort the comfortless, and to strengthen the weak, and relieve the thirsty souls. Oh, how sweet are *Shiloh's* brooks, where no galley with oars can pass, where the water of life flows softly, but sweetly, without any thing that flesh and blood can do, for that avails nothing in our heavenly journey, and, therefore, to be had in no reputation, but to be daily denied, and the cross taken up; and following Jesus faithfully and fully towards the crown, which is the blessed recompense for us to look unto, that we may run the race that is set before us in patience, that in the end we may obtain the mark of the prize of the high-calling that is in Christ Jesus, which is a mystery to those that do not obey him, but a sweet benefit to them that do obey his call; for they are chosen ones, a peculiar people, zealous of good works, glorifying our heavenly Father. And here we come to know that scripture fulfilled, where it is said *You shall call upon me in times of trouble and I will deliver, and you shall glorify me.*

Oh, that all the convinced ones, for whom I am so often concerned, would but consider, that all that are amongst us, might be of us, in glorifying God, by answering the divine requirings of his love; for we all know sufficient, but all do not obey; but yet the unfaithfulness of some does not make void the reward of the faithful, God forbid; but the reward encourages them to invite all to taste and see for themselves how good the Lord is; for he is communicating of fresh supplies of his tender love, and soul-refreshing life, undeclarably unto them that fear him, and dare not offend him, and so love him, as to keep his commands; them he will make partakers of his precious promises, for he promised never to leave nor forsake his, and to be with them at their down-lying and uprising, and at all times both day and night. As we keep covenant with him, he will be with us, and we shall be with him that lives for ever to give life to us, who wait upon him, and that we may have it more abundantly, that we may live to his praise, though amongst a crooked generation, who do daily provoke the righteous God. Surely the crying sins of the ungodly have long cried for vengeance in the ears of the mighty God of heaven and earth, and his just judgments will suddenly find them out; and then if *Daniel, Noah,* and *Lot* were there, they shall deliver none but their own souls! And, therefore, we have cause to be concerned as *Lot* was in *Sodom,* that we may be preachers of righteousness in our lives and conversations; that as the wicked do dishonour and grieve the Lord, we may be the more careful to honour and glorify him, by bringing forth much fruit, for his delight is in such; and if we abide in Christ Jesus, the true vine, then shall we be fruitful in every good work; for he is the root from whence we receive virtue, else we should wither and soon decay; but blessed be the root from whence we receive sap and daily relief. Oh, that it may lie always upon our branches, that we may bring forth fruit in due season, and blossom as the rose of *Sharon,* and grow as the lily of the valley, yielding a good savour in our words and actions, that whether together or asunder, we may be one another's joy and crown of rejoicing in the Lord Jesus, in whom our fresh springs are, who is the fountain of all our mercies, whose streams make glad his whole city, who relieves and replenishes our souls, and gives us many fruitful seasons, and makes our souls partakers of the early and latter rain, and of his eternal Spirit, wherein is the bond of peace, in which the Lord God of all our mercies, keep us all near unto himself, and one unto another, that, through the enjoyment of the same, we may magnify his eternal Power, and praise his most holy Name, for it is worthy to be honoured and renowned over all, and that for evermore. *Amen*, saith the soul of your dear sister, in that which reaches over sea and land.

JOAN VOKINS.

Written at *Drogheda*, in *Ireland*, the 27th of the 9th month, 1686.

Friends here are well, and in the enjoyment of peace and plenty, blessed be the Lord! and meetings large for the most part, and friends unanimously concerned in the service of Truth, as in the beginning, and keep their zeal for Truth, and delight to live in it.

Here follows a Paper that was printed in 1687, *entitled,*

A TENDER INVITATION UNTO ALL THOSE THAT WANT PEACE WITH GOD, BY REASON OF THE BURDEN OF SIN THAT KEEPS THEM FROM ACCEPTANCE WITH THE LORD JESUS, AND FROM AN ASSURANCE OF SALVATION, THOUGH IT BE VERY DESIRABLE TO THEM.

Oh, it is the weary and heavy-laden that he tenders rest unto! and they that take heed to his good Spirit which is light, and leave off that which it condemns, and follow its instructions, they obtain the way of life, and he becomes their Shepherd, and they hear his voice, and a stranger they will not hear; but they follow him; and he feeds them with that which the strangers to his voice, and hireling shepherds cannot attain unto, by all their arts or parts external; but it comes to be enjoyed by faith in Christ Jesus, that gives victory over sin; and, therefore, it is time for all people to consider, and as the apostle said, to try and examine themselves, whether they be in the true faith or no; for there is no true faith, but that which stands in the almighty Power, and that gives victory over the powers of darkness; and without this faith it is impossible to please God, as it is left upon record in the scriptures of Truth. So all are to believe in the Son of God, who is the Light of the world, and hath enlightened every one that comes into the world, as saith the scripture; and in the universal love of God, he gave his Son for a Light to enlighten the Gentiles, and to be salvation unto the ends of the earth. He died for all; and his love so far extended unto all, both male and female, that he would have none to perish, but that all by turning to his good Spirit, may be saved from all that the evil spirit leads into; for whosoever follows the leadings of the Spirit of Jesus, who is given for a Leader of his people, he leads them in the path of righteousness, and as they come to be servants of righteousness, they come to be free from sin. It is written in the scriptures of Truth, that the servants of sin are free from righteousness, and they that commit sin are of the devil, for he is the original of sin; but Jesus Christ is the original of the pure, holy and undefiled religion, that keeps from the evil of the world, which is pride, adultery, lying, cheating, idolatry, superstition, and other spots that those are stained with, who are not acquainted with him, that said, I wisdom lead in the midst of the paths of judgment, to cause them that love me to inherit substance. There is much talking of loving him, but few inclined to keep his commands; and much talking of his fear, but little standing in awe, so as not to offend him. But so far are many from taking heed unto the measure of his Spirit of Light that he hath placed in their hearts, that they do not know it leading them to the heart-cleansing fear; for if they did, how could they plead for sin, so long as they remain in these bodies? whereas it hath been said by the Spirit of the Lord, and left upon scripture record, that the fear of the Lord, is as a fountain of life, to depart from the snares of death; and the beginning of the true wisdom, and a good understanding, have all they that follow after it, for they depart from iniquity. It cleanses the heart, and keeps it clean, according to the testimonies the scriptures bear record of; therefore unto it I recommend all people, that all may have the privilege of it, that their hearts may be cleansed; for it is well known, there is no repentance in the grave, but as death leaves, righteous judgment will find. And, therefore, let the long-suffering and patience of the Lord lead to repentance, such a repentance that needs no repenting of, a changing of the heart, abstaining and refraining from every appearance of evil.

This is that which the Lord hath long waited for, and doth yet wait to be good and gracious unto all those that confess and forsake their evil thoughts, words, and works, and they shall surely find mercy with him, and be acquainted with him, and feel acceptance with him, and know the work of his sanctifying power, to sanctify throughout in body, soul, and spirit, that the work of sanctification may not be to do when the messenger of death will not be denied, for then it will be too late to work out our salvation with fear and trembling; and, therefore, it would be good for all to consider, how good the Lord is, in that he hath considered the frailty of all flesh, and hath given unto every one a measure of his good Spirit, to help our infirmities, and to teach us. But if we neglect this gift of God, we shall be inexcusable in the day of account, and he will be clear of us all; and, therefore, let all be diligent to hear the word of reconciliation, that the work thereof may be experienced, for it begets again unto God, those that were afar off, and when the work of regeneration is witnessed, and the birth of the water of life, and Spirit of Jesus; then the new creature that avails with God, comes to be in unity and peace with him, and then the Spirit of Jesus bears witness to the spirits of such, that they are the children of the Lord, but except a being born again, there can be no entering into the kingdom; for the first birth cannot enter into the first *Adam's* nature, all are dead, but they that are begotten again by the word of God's power, as the scripture testifies, they come to be changed into the nature of the second *Adam*, the Lord from heaven, the quickening Spirit, in him all such are made alive; and as they live in his fear, and do not grieve his Spirit, their sufficiency is in the engrafted Word of his Grace that is able to save, and in the same do witness preservation, as in the days of old; it is the same that *David* hid in his heart, that he might not sin against the Lord, and it was as a lantern unto his feet, and a light unto his path.

And so it is now, blessed be the Name of the Lord! unto them who are truly watchful in it. But those that are obeying the power of darkness, break the command of Christ Jesus; and it is left upon scripture record, that he did not say only unto one, but unto all, watch; and surely it is as needful as ever for us to keep a narrow watch, and that in the Light; for our soul's enemy works always in the dark, and except we keep a continual watch over our hearts, in that which doth discover his snares, we cannot escape; and so let all that have any sense, that it is their duty to wait upon the Lord, be careful to keep the command of watchfulness, that the enemy, nor any of his instruments, do not prevent from waiting in stillness upon the Lord, for he doth renew the strength of them that do truly wait upon him; and the Lord, by his servant, hath said, *That they shall run and not be weary, and walk and not faint;* and now he is fulfilling the scripture, wherein it is said, *The children of the Lord shall be taught of the Lord, and they shall be established in righteousness, and great shall be their peace.*

Oh, let all that want it, hearken unto the true Shepherd of the little flock, for whom the kingdom is prepared, who encourages them, and bids them fear not; though the wolfish destroyer is nigh unto them, yet he is the overseer, and in all trials and exercises he is their preservation; and they that have been exercised deeply, and tried thoroughly, they can tell of his wonderful works, and have cause to speak well of his most worthy Name, and to invite others to come and taste and see for themselves, how good the Lord is, in that he gives all a time of tender visitation. Oh! that all people would but consider it before it be too late, that while the good Spirit of Light is striving, their hearts may be affected with it, and joined to it, for it will not always strive; and, therefore, let such as could not come into obedience because of sufferings, now consider how good the Lord is, in that he hath calmed the storms of persecution, and opened a door for such as are convinced to come into obedience; let them now perform what they promised to the Lord, when they were looking to see what the Lord would do with his poor despised people, (called *Quakers*,) for, said they, it is the Truth that they suffer for, but we cannot suffer for it; the sufferings are too hard for us to bear, else we should own it. Oh! let all such truly consider the wonderful love of God, his tender mercy may not be disregarded, nor his great love undervalued, but let every such a one double their diligence, and make no delays, for delays in this weighty concern are very dangerous; for who knows how little time they have to come, or what it may bring forth; therefore, that the present time be not ill spent, *but while it is to day, if any will hear his voice, let them not harden their hearts, as it was in the day of provocation:* for many are the invitations of the great love of God, and if it be slighted, he will certainly withhold his mercies; and therefore we have great need to embrace his love, that we may not provoke him to wrath, for he is just, and will render unto all people according to their doings.

JOAN VOKINS.

West-Chawlow, 14th of the
3rd month, 1687.

A TESTIMONY TO THE WORK OF GOD'S POWER.

BECAUSE of the marvellous love of God in Christ Jesus, I cannot conceal my testimony for the wonderful work of his eternal Power, that hath been admirably manifested in my poor soul, and weak, frail body, and if I should not leave a short testimony of it to posterity, I should be very ungrateful. I pray God that the sin of ingratitude may not be laid heavy on any of us professing Truth, when the messenger of death calls, but that while we live we may live in subjection to his almighty Power, that when we die, we may seal our testimonies thereunto in true submission, and receive the blessed reward of the faithful.

Oh, what tongue can declare the wonderful loving-kindness of the Lord, as is experienced by those that obey his commands! Surely this is the way to abide in his love, and his great love has been so largely manifested to me, that it has engaged me so to love him again, as to forsake the world's glory, customs and fashions, vanities, elements, traditions, and superstitions, and to take up my daily cross and follow Jesus through the many tribulations. But blessed be his worthy Name! he hath filled my cup with his sweet consolations, and caused me to say, that one day in his courts, is better than a thousand elsewhere; and I had rather be a door-keeper in the house of my God, than to dwell in the pleasantest palace of the wicked. For until I through tender mercy, had unity with Jesus in his divine Spirit of Light, my soul could have no true satisfaction, though ever so self-righteous; but when the heart-searching Light made manifest my condition, my heart was so affected with it, that I still desired the operation of the power of it; and as I came to watch in the measure of it, I became aware of the enemy, and through faith in Christ Jesus obtained a waiting state, which could not be obtained by me, but as I felt the almighty Power to rebuke the subtle enemy that lies so nigh. As we are commanded to watch, we find great benefit by keeping that command. And magnified be that wonderful Power that has preserved in dangers deep, and difficulties many; there is nothing too hard for it to do; it has often rebuked the destroyer, helped the helpless, and strengthened the weak, and supported the needy; and as we have waited for it, we have been partakers of the arising of it, to our comfort, when our souls have been in a desolate condition, when we could not help ourselves, nor had none to help us. Oh! how hath it wrought by sea and land, and among false brethren; it hath so signally preserved and wrought deliverances many, sometimes by ways unexpected. Surely it is worthy to be trusted in, and depended upon, and magnified, as it hath been manifested, my soul hath cause to say to the honour and renown of it, for its perfect strength hath been my support in every great weakness, and in its strength I have travelled many thousands of miles by land, and many thousands of leagues by sea, through many and sore exercises, both inwardly and outwardly, and it hath raised my soul from death, and my body many times from the brink of the grave. Oh! let it have honour of its own works, saith my soul; for it is worthy, for it will make the strong to bow, and the weak to be as *David*, and it is worthy to be extolled in a wonderful manner, for no heart can be too much affected with it, there is all-sufficiency in it, to relieve the poor and to encourage the feeble. Though there be much to be met with in our heavenly progress, yet here is a sure defence in stormy times, wherein (glory unto it) I have found shelter, when many times in a weary condition by reason of exercise of soul and spirit, and weakness and pain of body. Oh! how many hundreds of miles have I travelled in this the land of my nativity, and thousands elsewhere, in such a condition, not having many well days in many years together, but yet have good cause to say, (to the honour and renown of the sanctifying Power of the God of my life,) blessed be the Lord Jesus, his rod and staff have comforted me, and he is always with me, and I have cause to admire the tender dealing of my heavenly Father, for he hath exercised me in the deep, and made his wonders known. And I have cause to speak well of his worthy Name, for it hath been as ointment poured into my poor wounded soul, and it was also so much comfort and strength to my weak body, that I can tenderly invite others to come and taste and see how good that Name is that brings salvation, that those that have a desire for it, may obtain it; for as the heart comes to be bowed unto the powerful Name of Jesus, and the soul and spirit come to be gathered into a sense of the great love of God, there will then be felt a necessity to serve and obey the God of all our mercies. And this was with me when in great weakness, when temptations came in as a flood, and the enemy, by his buffettings, was ready to overcome. Oh! blessed and magnified, and renowned over all, be that everlasting Power, that wrought a resignment so effectually, and caused me to cast my care upon him, that always careth for his children, who is the Holy One, and dwelleth in the highest heavens, and has regard to them of low degree, for he has been more to me than all that this world can produce, and hath fulfilled many precious scriptures. He hath not been wanting as a tender Father, but his mercies of old, and the continuation of his favours, and the renewing of his tender dealing, have deeply obliged me to glorify him unto the end, and in the end for evermore, for he is worthy, for he hath redeemed my soul from out of the grave of sin and death : and now may I say to the praise, and honour, and renown of his powerful Name, that to live is Christ, and to die is so much gain, that my soul is deeply affected in a true consideration of the same. Oh, that my posterity and friends, for whom my soul hath so long breathed and travailed may be so concerned, that every one may be made partakers of the like precious faith with me, while on the stage of this world, that we may leave a faithful testimony behind, that the generations to come may be induced thereby to fear and serve the Lord, for he is a sure rewarder of all them that are diligent in so doing, not only in this world, but in that which is to come, with life everlasting, world without end. *Amen.*

JOAN VOKINS.

This was written a few months before her decease, about the 1st month, 1690.

TO WILLIAM COOPER AND HIS WIFE, DWELLING IN WEST JERSEY, NEAR DELAWARE RIVER, NOT FAR FROM BURLINGTON. THESE ARE

DEAR and tender friends, *William Cooper* and *M.*, my love in the unchangeable Truth salutes you, and in the same I still desire your welfare as my own, with all that hold fast their integrity, and retain their first love, they are as near and dear unto me as ever, and my entire love truly reaches to them all. I desire thou mayst let them know, if they have received my letters and epistles, for I have sent several, but my kinsman dying by the way, makes me question whether what I sent did ever come to any of your hands; for I sent to you, and to *S. Spicer*, and *Lydia Wright*, (as was,) and to her husband, and to her sister *Mary Andrews*, and to several others in *Pennsylvania* side, as well as on that side, and I should be very glad to hear of your welfare in the Lord Jesus, for that my soul still travails as truly as when I was amongst you. Oh, that your faithfulness and living obedience may engage our heavenly Father to answer the breathing desires of my soul, for you in those remote places, for I cannot forget you. The cry often runs through me for your preservation and prosperity every way, and that the honour of Truth and the good one of another may be preferred far more than all other things, that our nearness and dearness unto our tender God, and one unto another may be felt and witnessed, that we may praise his worthy Name, and magnify his preserving and delivering power, for it hath been largely manifested, may a little remnant truly say, that has known the wonderful works of our God to admiration. Oh, we have great cause to speak well of his Name, to remember his mercies of old, and to hold the continuation of his favours in great esteem! Blessed be the Lord Jesus, he hath not been wanting to us, but his renewed mercies daily are sufficient to deeply engage us to renew our faithfulness and obedience, that our heavenly Father may be pleased to continue and multiply his tender dealings towards us, that whatever is yet to come, may never be able to separate us from the sense of his love, from the seasonedness of his holy fear, or from that cementing life, that joins us as members unto Christ our Head. And that if trials should abound, we may all feel the love and life of Jesus to superabound, that every bitter cup that is yet to come may be sweetened, all hard things made easy, and we encouraged to travel on in our heavenly progress, keeping a narrow watch in the precious Light, and diligently waiting in the same, that we may be filled with heavenly treasure, for all other is very uncertain. We here do meet with a sufficient share of many and variable exercises; neither do I expect, that you there do go free; but this is that I do desire above all things, even your living growth in the precious Truth, and that you may endure to the end; for they are assuredly happy, and a blessed reward is prepared for them! And in a living sense of the same, the Lord God of our lives keep us here, and you there, that our breathings may be continued one for another, that we may be refreshed one in another, and praise the God of heaven and earth together, (in his one eternal Spirit,) as with one heart and soul, for he is worthy to be had in living remembrance, and his pure Power to be magnified and renowned over all. Unto it I commit us all, for it is over all, and worthy to have the disposing of us all; and with it I leave all, for there is nothing too hard for it to do; it is worthy to be exalted over all in heaven and earth, and that for evermore, saith the soul of your loving sister in the unchangeable Truth,

JOAN VOKINS.

London, 28th of the
4th month, 1690.

POSTSCRIPT.

At this season, as at many other times, our General Meeting here, has been a time of very precious heavenly bedewings. Blessed be the God of heaven and earth, his Power has filled the assemblies of his people! and the remembrance of you and other remote islands is signified by epistles that were signed at our women's meetings, and ordered to be sent to you, when opportunity presents, that you may rejoice with us, and joy in the God of your and our salvation, in and through Christ Jesus, who lives and abides to make intercession for us, his poor helpless ones, who have had no helper but him. Oh, glory to his Name for ever, he has been with us in many troubles, and gives us cause to believe he will be with us for ever! And unto his tender care do I commit all our states and conditions, for fresh and suitable supplies come from him the fountain of all our mercies, to whom be returned the honour and the glory over all, for he is worthy for evermore.

The Lord my God, in his great goodness to me, (after a long time of weakness,) has enabled me by his Power, to come once more to this Yearly Meeting, to be refreshed among his worthy ones, and I could do no less than cast my mite into the treasury. And when the epistle comes, as is directed, to *West* and *East Jersey* and *Philadelphia*, I entreat thee and thy wife to let copies be sent to *York* and *Long Island*. J. V.

TO ANTIGUA AND NEVIS, &c.

G. W., DEAR FRIEND, after the salutation of my dear love, which truly reaches unto thee, thy wife, and friends, this is to let you know, that I cannot forget you in those remote islands, but have been often concerned for you in a travail of soul before the Lord, and now having this opportunity (after a long time of bodily weakness) to visit friends at *London,* I can do no less than let you know, that, through tender mercy, I am yet alive, to tell of the goodness of the Lord, to admire the works of his almighty Power, and to speak well of his worthy Name. For glory and honour and praises thereunto, he is the same as ever, and his mercies, and the continuation of his favours, are never to be forgotten, and his renewed goodness and mercies, both spiritual and temporal, are daily sufficient to engage us to renew our faithfulness and obedience unto our tender God. Oh, that thus it may be with all that he has been so good unto, as to bring near unto himself and one unto another, who were once afar off from the fellowship of the saints in Light! But blessed be the Lord, who hath caused his Light to shine in our tabernacles, and showed us the way that we should walk in. And now Christ Jesus is our life and salvation, and he fills our cups with sweet consolation; and as many as do walk in the Light have fellowship one with another, and the blood of Jesus Christ cleanses from all sin, and purifies and fits the earthen vessel for the heavenly treasure. And the excellency of the Power is of the Lord, and the glory over all is his, and he is near unto them that seek his glory more than their outward interest, and he will fill their treasuries with this heavenly treasure, and so as we follow him, we inherit substance, and have no more need to wander, as in the days past, after husks and shadows, but to keep to the Shepherd and Bishop of our souls; for blessed be his Name, he feeds us in the green pastures of life, and causes us to lie down by the still waters, when the raging sea foams out mire and dirt. Oh, this is he that led *Israel* in the days of old, and never said to the seed of *Jacob, Seek ye my face in vain.* And therefore, dear friends, we have cause to say, to the praise of his holy Name, *That goodly are the tents of Jacob, and blessed is his dwelling-place;* for it is within the munition of rocks, where our bread is ever sure, and the water of life never fails, where the weary find sweet repose, and the thirsty are refreshed, and where our souls feed together, when our bodies are far asunder. So therein the Lord preserve us and you unto the end, that he may have the honour, and our souls the benefit for evermore.

And by this thou mayst know, that we have had a precious time here at *London*, at our Yearly Meeting, and many precious testimonies have been borne by sons and daughters, to the almighty Power of God, that hath filled the assemblies of his people. Oh, how hath the heavenly dew distilled upon our branches, and brought forth fruit that reaches unto you in those islands! I dearly desire it may be pleasant to your taste, that we may be refreshed one in another, and be one another's joy and rejoicing in the Lord Jesus; and that the epistles of love that were signed here at our Yearly and Quarterly Meetings, may induce you to write again, that you there, may have a correspondence with friends here, in the work and service that our God hath called us unto, that Spiritual fruits may be brought forth and abound in all the churches. Our heavenly Father delights in those that bring forth the fruits of his Spirit, for every member that bringeth forth fruit to his praise, he purges and waters with the seasons of his early and latter rain, and causes them to bring forth fruit more and more. And so the dew of the everlasting hills rest upon you, and us, and upon all the heritage of God everywhere, for evermore. *Amen,* saith the soul of thy true friend and sister, in that which reaches over sea and land, and which length of time cannot wear out.

JOAN VOKINS.

I hope to hear from *Nevis,* as opportunity presents. My dear love is to *W. Fifill's* widow, if yet alive, and to all the rest of those that are alive, who love the Truth and live in it, for they are very precious to me. J. V.

At *London.*
This was written soon after the Yearly Meeting, 1690, about the end of the 4th, or the beginning of the 5th month, 1690.

THE END.

www.ingramcontent.com/pod-product-compliance
Lightning Source LLC
Chambersburg PA
CBHW030331170426
43202CB00010B/1092